THE FOURTEENTH AMENDMENT AND THE NEGRO SINCE 1920

THE FOURTEENTH AMENDMENT AND THE NEGRO SINCE 1920

BY

BERNARD H. NELSON, M.A.

NEW YORK / RUSSELL & RUSSELL

REISSUED, 1967, BY RUSSELL & RUSSELL
A DIVISION OF ATHENEUM HOUSE, INC.
BY ARRANGEMENT WITH BERNARD H. NELSON
L. C. CATALOG CARD NO: 66-27131

SUBMITTED TO THE FACULTY OF THE GRADUATE SCHOOL OF ARTS AND SCIENCES OF THE CATHOLIC UNIVERSITY OF AMERICA IN PARTIAL FULFILLMENT OF THE REQUIREMENTS FOR THE DEGREE OF DOCTOR OF PHILOSOPHY

CONTENTS

PREFACE

One constitutional result of the Civil War was the addition of three amendments to the Constitution of the United States which implicitly concerned the Negro. Of these three amendments, the Fourteenth has been of greatest importance in both the constitutional history of the United States and the history of the Negro race in America. This amendment was projected and passed with the design of securing and protecting the Negro in the rights of freedom and citizenship. Except for the years immediately following the Civil War, in no era has it been more difficult to protect the rights and privileges of minority groups, the Negro among them, than in the decades of the twenties and thirties. These were decades of national crisis and readjustment in which the rights of minorities were sometimes disregarded as the nation attempted to meet problems inherent in post-war readjustment and the depression.

During the period of this investigation, no specialized study of the Fourteenth Amendment and the Negro, dealing with the period 1920–1943, has come to the writer's notice. It should be noted, however, that some aspects of the subject have been treated in various articles and published investigations of the past seven years. Most notable among the latter are the published studies by Charles S. Mangum and Henry J. McGuinn. An examination of these investigations revealed that they differ in both scope and treatment from the present study.

This study is an attempt to examine the interpretation and application of the Fourteenth Amendment between 1920 and 1943 to determine its effectiveness in protecting the rights and privileges of the Negro citizen. To a great extent, therefore, this investigation is primarily concerned with the Fourteenth Amendment, the Negro, and American courts. But any attempt to determine the interpretation of the amendment without giving some notice to social and political developments of the period, which of necessity influenced judicial interpretation, would deprive this study of an essential dimension. Thus, an attempt has been made to determine the impact of these developments upon the interpretation and application of the amendment in matters affecting the Negro.

The chief sources for this study are sixty-nine cases, decided between 1920 and 1943, involving the Fourteenth Amendment and the Negro. The *Fourth Decennial Digest* and the *Federal Digest* were thoroughly searched for all cases bearing on the subject. Each case was read to determine the issue involved, the clause of the Fourteenth Amendment invoked, and the particular interpretation given, or application made by the court. Actions resulting in memorandum decisions or consent decrees have been generally omitted because they involved interpretations or applications already established by the courts.

The writer is greatly indebted to the General Education Board of New York City for fellowship awards in 1943 and 1944 which presented the opportunity to undertake and complete this investigation. The invaluable direction and guidance given by Professor Richard J. Purcell, from the time the study was projected to its completion, can never be sufficiently acknowledged. To Sister Marie Carolyn Klinkhamer, O.P., Ph.D., the writer is grateful for reading the manuscript and making valuable suggestions and criticisms. Particular mention is made of the assistance given by Mrs. Dorothy Porter, Curator of the Moreland Collection, Howard University, in granting permission to use the Negro newspaper files and materials in that Collection.

CHAPTER I

THE HISTORICAL SETTING

No part of the Constitution of the United States has been the source of as much litigation as the Fourteenth Amendment; and no one of the three " Negro Amendments " has been invoked by the Negro as frequently as the Fourteenth Amendment. With much justification, a constitutional historian writing over forty years ago remarked: " Our constitutional history is largely a commentary upon the Fourteenth Amendment." [1] Conceived in a burst of idealism, fear and confusion, and declared a part of the organic law of the land on July 28, 1868, this amendment was to be the Negro's charter of liberty—a bulwark of protection against inequality and discriminatory treatment in the states. Since 1868 it has been in the Fourteenth Amendment that the Negro, as well as other minority groups, has sought Federal protection for the fundamental rights of American citizenship.

Many and varied have been the motives and objectives attributed to those who framed the amendment and the Congress which passed it.[2] It appears that the framing and adoption of the Fourteenth Amendment were directly influenced by the desire to punish the South,[3] to assure continued control of the government by the Republican party, and to limit the police power of the states. However, it seems apparent that those who directed its passage [4]

[1] William P. Guthrie, *The Fourteenth Article of Amendment to the Constitution of the United States* (Boston, 1898), 3.

[2] Charles S. Mangum, *The Legal Status of the Negro* (Chapel Hill, N. C., 1940), 27; Charles W. Collins, *The Fourteenth Amendment and the States* (Boston, 1912), 9–12; James G. Blaine, *Twenty Years of Congress* (Norwich, Conn., 1886), II, 188–92; John W. Burgess, *Reconstruction and the Constitution* (New York, 1902), 74.

[3] Blaine, *op. cit.,* II, 212–13, held that the resolution of amendment as adopted by Congress " was not as severe as the leaders would have liked it."

[4] Authorship of the Fourteenth Amendment has been ascribed to different persons. Among them are Judge Stephen Neale and Robert Dale Owen, both

were intent upon increasing the rights and privileges of the recently emancipated Negro and upon assuring him freedom from oppression and equality before the law. From this point of view, the Fourteenth Amendment was a logical supplement to the Thirteenth Amendment; it gave protection to that freedom which the Thirteenth Amendment had already bestowed. This aim, whether immediate or ultimate, was implemented by making the Bill of Rights applicable to the states and by so restricting their exercise of power as to compel them to respect the fundamental guarantees of life, liberty, and property in regard to all citizens.[5]

Many of the supporters of the amendment felt that its principal purpose was to confer additional rights and immunities upon members of the Negro race.[6] This became necessary when the sentiment which had produced the Black Codes in the southern states threatened to nullify the Thirteenth Amendment. In its early decisions on the Fourteenth Amendment, the Supreme Court held this to be its main purpose. The Court declared the amendment was designed to raise the Negro " into perfect equality of civil rights with all other persons " [7] and " to protect [him] from the oppression of the white man." [8]

Prominent among the purposes of the Fourteenth Amendment, one which was to lead to a great deal of legal controversy in the two decades, 1920–1940, was that of enfranchising the Negro. Charles Sumner urged the enfranchisement of the Negro in the Senate debates on the amendment. Negro suffrage was a necessity, he observed, " for the sake of the public security and public faith " and would prove " a peacemaker, a schoolmaster, [and] a

---

of Indiana. However, the evidence points to Senator John A. Bingham as the author of Section I. See Horace E. Flack, *The Adoption of the Fourteenth Amendment* (Baltimore, 1908), 69–71.

[5] *Ibid.*, 98.

[6] Lyman Windolph, " Two Fourteenth Amendments," *Annals of the American Academy of Political and Social Science,* CXCV (1938), 264–68.

[7] *Ex parte Virginia,* 100 U. S. 339 (1879); also *Strauder v. West Virginia,* 100 U. S. 303 (1879).

[8] *Slaughter House Cases,* 16 Wallace 36 (1873). The narrow view of Mr. Justice Miller in these cases, that the equal protection clause was confined exclusively to discriminatory state action against Negroes, was severely criticized and later abandoned.

protector."[9] Without the ballot for the freedmen both the Union and the cause of human rights would be imperiled.[10] In the opinion of one author, the movement for Negro suffrage was the most influential of all the movements which influenced or inspired the amendment.[11]

Congressional leaders were deeply concerned over the increased representation and political power which the southern states would wield as a result of the emancipation of the Negro. The first attempt to secure Negro suffrage was the suggestion to exclude all members of any race from the basis of representation whenever a state denied the franchise to any member of that race on account of race or color.[12] This proved unacceptable to Congress as too cumbersome, and it was replaced by Section 2 as now found in the amendment which penalizes a state for restricting the sufrage on account of race or color. Charges of political partisanship and the desire to utilize the Negro vote to control the South were made when Section 2 was inserted in the amendment; and Republican leaders had to refute such charges for many years.[13]

Whatever the ulterior motive or interest in Negro suffrage, the Congress which passed the Fourteenth Amendment felt that it had so penalized the restriction of the franchise, on racial grounds, that the Negro would be permitted to function effectively as a voter. The evidence hardly permits one to believe other than that one of the foremost purposes of the Fourteenth Amendment was to secure the Negro in the right to vote.

Any consideration of the aims or purposes of the Fourteenth Amendment must give some notice to its intent as far as corporations are concerned. Corporations have been so successful in securing protection under this amendment against state action[14]

[9] Quoted in Blaine, *op. cit.,* II, 199.

[10] Carl M. Frasure, "Charles Sumner and the Rights of the Negro," *Journal of Negro History,* XIII (1938), 134.

[11] Joseph B. James, *Framing the Fourteenth Amendment* (Urbana, Ill., 1939), 6.

[12] Blaine, *op. cit.,* II, 195–96.

[13] See the letter of George S. Boutwell to the Boston *Herald,* May 19, 1900, quoted in Richard P. Hollowell, *Why the Negro Was Enfranchised* (Boston, 1903), 12, which offers a refutation of this charge.

[14] Charles W. Collins, *The Fourteenth Amendment and the States,* 183,

that students have sought to ascertain the intent of the framers in this respect. The "conspiracy theory," that "laboring ostensibly in the interests of the freedmen . . . the astute Republican lawyers who made up the majority of the Committee had intentionally used language . . . which gave corporations . . . generally increased judicial protection as against state legislatures," [15] is the product of this investigation. This theory views the drafting process as something of an intrigue.

Roscoe Conkling and John A. Bingham, both members of the Reconstruction Committee, are pictured as largely responsible for bringing corporations under the protection of the Fourteenth Amendment. It is held that their influence caused the substitution of the word "persons" for the word "citizens" in Section 1 of the amendment.[16] Later, in the *San Mateo County* case, Conkling held that it was the committee's intent to protect companies, as well as individuals, against discriminatory state action.[17] This contention appears to be unsupported by the evidence; for though the corporation was mentioned in the discussions on the amendment, no special significance appears to have been attached to this infant business organization.[18] Whatever protection corporations have secured under the amendment has more likely been won by the perversion of the framers' true intent,[19] which has given the amendment a construction not intended in 1868.

The Supreme Court was called upon to interpret the Fourteenth Amendment for the first time in 1873, five years after its adoption. Numerous questions had to be answered: What was its scope? What rights and privileges did it confer? What was the scope of Congressional power under the amendment? These

---

points out that of 604 cases decided by the Supreme Court on the Fourteenth Amendment from 1873 to 1910, twenty-eight involved the Negro while 313 involved corporations.

15 Howard J. Graham, "The Conspiracy Theory of the Fourteenth Amendment," 47 *Yale Law Journal,* 372.

16 Louis B. Boudin, "Truth and Fiction About the Fourteenth Amendment," 16 *New York University Law Quarterly,* 19–30.

17 Guthrie, *op. cit.,* 25.

18 Andrew C. McLaughlin, "The Court, the Corporation, and Conkling," *American Historical Review,* XLVI (1944), 50.

19 *Ibid.* See also Boudin, *loc. cit.,* 67.

questions were answered by the Court in its decisions prior to 1920. The rules established in many of these early decisions were applied and determined the outcome of many cases involving the Negro before the courts during the period treated in this study.

The first cases to come before the Supreme Court under the Fourteenth Amendment, while not involving a Negro litigant, resulted in a decision which indicated the narrow interpretation the Court would adopt in cases which invoked its guarantees. In these cases, known as the *Slaughter House* cases,[20] the Court ruled that the Fourteenth Amendment offered no protection for ordinary civil rights; it held that the due process of law clause effected no limitation on the state's police power.[21] Only the privileges and immunities of citizens of the United States, in contrast with citizens of the states, were protected. These privileges and immunities the Court did not or would not, at that time, enumerate.[22]

To secure Negroes in the rights of citizenship, Congress had enacted the Civil Rights Act, in 1875, under authority of the Fourteenth Amendment.[23] This measure demanded equal accommodations for Negroes, without distinction because of race or color, in inns, public places, places of amusement, and public conveyances. The constitutionality of this act was at issue in the *Civil Rights* cases.[24] The Supreme Court decided that Congress had exceeded its power in enacting the measure. Only state action came within the prohibitions of the Fourteenth Amendment; it had no reference to the actions of individuals, no matter how discriminatory those actions might be. Discrimination at the

---

[20] 16 Wallace 36 (1873).

[21] Charles Warren, *The Supreme Court in United States History* (Boston, 1935), II, 538, discusses the implications and influences of this decision upon the Court's application of the amendment during the next half century.

[22] In *Minor v. Happersett,* 21 Wallace 162 (1874), the Court held that the Fourteenth Amendment did not add to the privileges and immunities guaranteed by the Constitution.

[23] United States, *Statutes-at-Large,* XVIII, 375. For a discussion of the act see Ellis P. Oberholtzer, *A History of the United States since 1865* (New York, 1937), III, 96.

[24] 109 U. S. 1 (1883).

hands of private persons could not be forbidden by congressional enactment under this amendment.

In a lengthy dissenting opinion of thirty-four pages, Mr. Justice Harlan refused to follow the reasoning of the majority. He felt that the Fourteenth Amendment conferred upon Congress the power to protect the citizen against discrimination at the hands of corporations and individuals charged with duties to the public, as well as that which resulted from state action. The Court's opinion, he stated, tended " to defeat the end [which] the people desire to accomplish, which they attempted to accomplish, and which they thought they had accomplished by changes in their fundamental law." [25] Later writers have considered the majority opinion as disregarding the intent and purpose of the framers of the amendment in this respect.[26]

A great deal of discriminatory anti-Chinese legislation was enacted by the state of California between 1870 and 1890. Cases testing the constitutionality of this legislation before Federal courts [27] resulted in the establishment of rules which were later applied in litigation involving the Negro. In one of these cases which invoked the guarantees of the Fourteenth Amendment, the Supreme Court ruled that the application, as well as the intent of legislation, must be considered in determining whether there had been a denial of equal protection of the law. Though a law is fair and impartial in appearance, if it is so administered as to result in an " illegal discrimination between persons in similar circumstances," then that denial of equal justice is prohibited by the Fourteenth Amendment.[28]

With the close of the Civil War, segregation laws designed to separate the races in schools, public places, and public conveyances were enacted by southern states. The constitutionality of legislation of this character was questioned after the adoption of the

---

[25] *Ibid.*, 26.

[26] Collins, *op. cit.*, 22; C. G. Woodson, "Fifty Years of Negro Citizenship as Qualified by the United States Supreme Court," *Journal of Negro History,* VI (1921), 11–15; Flack, *op. cit.*, 7.

[27] Elmer C. Sandmeyer, " California Anti-Chinese Legislation and the Federal Courts," *Pacific Historical Review,* V (1936), 189–211.

[28] *Yick Wo v. Hopkins,* 118 U. S. 373 (1885).

Fourteenth Amendment, for it appeared that these enactments denied privileges and rights which the amendment guaranteed. Legislation establishing separate schools for the two races was contested under both the privileges and immunities and the equal protection clauses. In the case of *United States v. Buntin,*[29] a United States Circuit Court held that educational privileges were privileges granted by the state rather than by the United States. Whether or not separate schools would be established was a purely discretionary matter for the state to decide; however, where separate schools were established, an " equality of right " as distinguished from an " identity of right " must be maintained. So long as educational advantages for Negroes were, in all respects, " substantially equal " to those provided for whites, no denial of equal protection resulted.[30] When the issue was finally presented to the Supreme Court, the rule of the *Buntin* case was upheld. The Court reasoned that education was a concern of the state and that " only in the case of a clear and unmistakable disregard of rights " would the federal authority interfere with the management of schools.[31]

Between 1882 and 1898, the lower Federal courts generally upheld state segregation laws in regard to public carriers. These decisions most often took the position that the demand for separate cars for white and Negro passengers was merely a proper exercise of state police powers. Separation was legal so long as accommodations provided for Negro passengers were equal to those provided for whites.[32] This question was presented to the Supreme Court of the United States for the first time in the case of *Plessy v. Ferguson.*[33] Plessy, a Negro, purchased a first-class ticket on an eastern Louisiana railroad (an intra-state railroad).

---

29 10 Fed. 30 (U. S. C. C., Ohio, 1882).

30 In the case of *Wong Him v. Callahan,* 119 Fed. 381 (U. S. C. C., Calif., 1902), this rule was applied to persons of Mongolian descent.

31 *Cummings v. Richmond County Board of Education,* 175 U. S. 528 (1899).

32 *Gray v. Cincinnati and Southern Railroad Company,* 11 Fed. 683 (U. S. C. C., Ohio, 1882) ; *Murphy v. Western and Atlantic Railroad,* 23 Fed. 137 (U. S. C. C., Tenn., 1885) ; *Hank v. Southern Pacific Railroad Company,* 38 Fed. 226 (U. S. C. C., Tex., 1888).

33 163 U. S. 537 (1896).

He refused to accept a seat in a coach assigned to Negro passengers and was arrested and convicted of violating a Louisiana statute of 1890 which made it mandatory for all railroads operating in the state to provide separate coaches for Negro and white passengers.

The constitutionality of the Louisiana statute was questioned. It was contended that the enforcement of the statute resulted in an inequality which was prohibited by the Fourteenth Amendment. The Supreme Court held that the right for which protection was sought was a social right, not a legal right; and the Fourteenth Amendment did not force social equality which the commingling of the races implied. Laws requiring the separation of the races were within the competency of the state in the exercise of its police powers. In so far as such laws were intended to promote the public good and maintain peace and order, they were not unreasonable; and they neither abridged the citizen's privileges and immunities, nor denied him equal protection of the law.[34]

The line of reasoning and position taken by the Court was unacceptable to Justice Harlan. He wrote a dissenting opinion in which he urged the unconstitutionality of laws separating the races in public carriers. Such enactments he considered unconstitutional in that they interfered with the citizen's personal freedom "under the guise of giving equal accommodations to whites and blacks." Moreover, they fostered ideas of caste and inferiority. Such a ruling as that handed down by the Court permitted the regulation of the enjoyment of civil rights, solely on the basis of color, despite the fact that:

> Our Constitution is color-blind, and neither knows nor tolerates classes among citizens. . . . The law regards man as man, and takes no regard of his surroundings or of his color when his civil rights as guaranteed by the supreme law of the land are invoked. . . .[35]

[34] *Ibid.*, 543, 550.

[35] *Ibid.*, 556. Justice Harlan had been a staunch Unionist during the Civil War, though he was a Kentuckian. His nomination to the Court was held up for more than a month because of the "judicial ambitions" of leading senators. See Cortez A. M. Ewing, *Judges of the Supreme Court, 1789–1937* (Minneapolis, 1938), 23–24.

Furthermore, the majority decision would stimulate further aggression upon the rights of the Negro. The rules pronounced by the courts involving state segregation laws during this early period have remained the law in such matters.

Another effort to separate the races was made by some states through legislation forbidding either Negroes or whites to establish residences in blocks where a majority of the residences were inhabited by members of the other race. The Supreme Court was called upon to pass on the validity of such legislation in 1917 in the case of *Buchanan v. Warley*.[36] The case involved the residential segregation ordinance passed by Louisville, Kentucky, in 1914, and which had already been upheld by the state courts.[37] Nationwide attention was focused on the case before the Court because of the growing interest in some sections in legislation of this type.[38] It should be noted that similar legislation, directed against Mongolians and Mexicans, had been enacted by states of the Southwest and Pacific coast.

The Supreme Court ruled that the Louisville ordinance was an unjustifiable exercise of state police power which contravened the guarantees of the Fourteenth Amendment. While state authority might properly restrict the occupancy of property for reasons of public welfare, such restriction is not permissible when made solely on account of race or color. No matter what problems might arise from the habitation of Negroes and whites in close proximity, "their solution cannot be promoted by depriving citizens of their constitutional rights." [39] Thus, colored persons had a right to purchase, use, and dispose of property without discrimination by law, on account of race or color.

After the Civil War southern states continued the practice followed during the slave era of excluding Negroes from participation in the state judicial system. Exclusive administration of southern courts by whites, whose prejudices and preconceptions as

[36] 245 U. S. 60.

[37] See 165 Kentucky 556 (1916).

[38] National Association for the Advancement of Colored People, *Fifteenth Annual Report,* 1924 (New York, 1925), 5. Hereafter cited as N. A. A. C. P., *Annual Report.*

[39] 245 U. S. 80, 81.

to the Negro's proper place in southern society influenced their decisions, frequently resulted in injustice to Negro defendants before the courts. The practice of systematically excluding Negroes from service on grand and petit juries in the South was especially obnoxious in this respect, and it lent itself to the dispensation of unequal justice.[40] Numerous cases were brought before the United States Supreme Court between 1879 and 1920 in an effort to end the practice.

In early cases which involved the exclusion of Negroes from jury service, the Supreme Court held that when such discrimination was countenanced by state statute, it constituted a contravention of the Fourteenth Amendment.[41] Whether the exclusion resulted from the action of the legislature, executive, administrative officials, or courts was inconsequential; such discrimination was forbidden by law.[42] But the mere failure to include the names of Negro citizens on lists from which jurors were drawn, in the absence of state law excluding Negroes from jury service, was declared not in itself a denial of equal protection of law under the Fourteenth Amendment.[43] The burden of proof to establish the existence of an actual discrimination on racial grounds was placed upon the appellant. Proof of such discrimination could be established "only by proof overcoming denial on the part of the state."[44] The absence of such proof was held to be fatal to the charge of discrimination. In applying this rule the Court did not take into account the fact that possibilities were great that exclusion on racial grounds could be effected without the petitioner's being able to produce any evidence that would convince the Court.

Cases involving the Negro and the Fourteenth Amendment, which came before the United States Supreme Court between 1879 and 1920, reveal a conservative attitude on the part of the Court.

---

[40] Gilbert T. Stephenson, *Race Distinctions in American Law* (New York, 1911), 253–71.

[41] *Strauder v. West Virginia,* 100 U. S. 303 (1879). This rule was later applied in *Virginia v. Rives,* 100 U. S. 31 (1879), and in *Neale v. Delaware,* 103 U. S. 370 (1880).

[42] *Carter v. Texas,* 177 U. S. 442 (1899).

[43] *Smith v. State of Mississippi,* 162 U. S. 592 (1895); *Bush v. Commonwealth of Kentucky,* 107 U. S. 370 (1882).

[44] *Martin v. Texas,* 200 U. S. 321 (1906).

Conservative interpretation and narrow application of the amendment all but negated the "congressional ideal" of 1866–1868 and rendered the Fourteenth Amendment a most ineffective guarantee of civil liberty and equal justice under law. As a result, "the Negro was hindered economically, segregated socially, and his suffrage left unguarded politically."[45] The rule in the *Civil Rights* cases[46] had held that the Fourteenth Amendment offered protection only against state action and not against that of individuals or combinations of individuals in the states. Thus, there was provided at best only a partial immunity against trespass upon civil liberty and denial of equal justice. The interpretation of the amendment by the Supreme Court during this early period seemed to restrict narrowly the powers of Congress to enforce the amendment, in a positive way, with appropriate legislation.[47] The two basic doctrines, that the amendment did not operate directly upon the people and that Congress did not have the power to make positive and affirmative laws for its enforcement, left Congress with virtually no power to enforce the amendment.

There were some who saw in the Court's interpretation of the Fourteenth Amendment during the early period a return to the doctrine of states' rights. Said one authority in criticism of the rule that the amendment offered protection only against state action and not against that of individuals:

> I contend that this is no satisfactory solution of the problem [of civil liberty] . . . because sound political science requires that the entire individual immunity shall be defined, in principle, in the national constitution and shall have the fundamental guarantees of its defense in that constitution. . . . It is a resurrection of the doctrine of States' rights, in the extreme, when the Supreme Court of the United States put the interpretation which it did upon the new amendments. . . .[48]

[45] Thelma D. Ackiss, "The Negro and the Supreme Court to 1900," unpublished master's thesis, Howard University, 1936, 106.

[46] *Supra,* 5.

[47] Collins, *op. cit.,* 21; Woodson, *loc. cit.,* 14; Charles Warren, *The Supreme Court in United States History,* II, 600–16; James G. Blaine, *Twenty Years of Congress,* II, 419.

[48] John W. Burgess, "Present Problems of Constitutional Law," *Political Science Quarterly,* XIX (1904), 573.

Without question the decisions in cases prior to 1900 deprived the amendment of the great powers which the Congress thought it had securely placed in it,[49] and left a large control of civil liberty in the hands of the states. This result was no doubt welcomed in the South where public sentiment had opposed the adoption of the Fourteenth Amendment and the federal interference which that amendment entailed.

Cases brought to the Supreme Court by or in the interest of Negroes were generally decided against them for various reasons; [50] sometimes these reasons were extremely technical. However, it might be safely asserted that these decisions properly reflected the sentiment of the times.[51] By 1900 the North had adopted an attitude of "hands-off" as far as the question of Negro rights and the enforcement of the Fourteenth Amendment were concerned. Northern interest was too much absorbed by industrial expansion and consolidation to give much consideration to these questions.

On the other hand, the South had been alarmed over "imminent threats of social equality" ever since the adoption of the amendment. There was a conscious desire to exclude Negroes from any status that could be interpreted as a status of equality with whites. In the Fourteenth Amendment the southerner could observe far-reaching dangers; therefore, the amendment was unacceptable to him. A Georgian wrote: "Nothing possibly can come of such monstrous folly [equality of the Negro] but suffering and sorrow." Efforts to enforce the amendment, he stated, would produce "con-

---

[49] See Blaine, *op. cit.*, II, 419-20, for a detailed treatment of this point of view.

[50] Charles S. Mangum, *The Legal Status of the Negro*, 400. A compilation of Supreme Court decisions on the Fourteenth Amendment to 1910 by Charles W. Collins, *The Fourteenth Amendment and the States*, 68, reveals that of twenty-eight cases involving the Negro, twenty-two were decided against him.

[51] Frank Drake, "The Negro Before the Supreme Court," 66 *Albany Law Journal*, 247, feels that the extinction of the Negro's civil and political rights was "coeval with the reaction of public sentiment from its tone when the Civil War made the Negro race virtual wards of the national government." See also Kelly Miller, "Government and the Negro," *Annals of the American Academy of Political and Social Science*, CXL (1928), 160.

stantly recurring and extra legal methods of control."[52] The restraint and control which diversity in laws made possible were necessary for the orderly government of Negroes.[53] A somewhat similar sentiment was expressed by Governor Vardaman of Mississippi, who urged that "we must sweep the horizon of expedients to find a way around" this amendment until its repeal.[54] Public sentiment in the South was adverse to any broad interpretation of the amendment. No other conclusion can be drawn but that public sentiment, North and South, permitted the adoption of a conservative interpretation and a narrow application of the Fourteenth Amendment. However, in following the dictates of either conservatism or disinterestedness, the Supreme Court was charged with inconsistency and making use of sophistry in an effort to support southern aristocracy.[55] It was feared that so much of the liberal provisions of the Constitution had been stricken therefrom and so much "caste and autocracy" read into it by the Court's illiberal decisions that both discontent and radicalism must be the ultimate result.[56]

As the Fourteenth Amendment was interpreted and applied in regard to the Negro prior to 1920, considered from the point of view of the protection of the Negro's rights of citizenship, it must be declared a failure. In the first place, it was difficult to get cases involving the denial of Negroes' rights before Federal courts; and it was especially difficult to get the Supreme Court to accept jurisdiction in such cases. In all, only twenty-eight cases involving the Negro and the Fourteenth Amendment were decided by the Supreme Court between 1868 and 1910; and of this number

---

52 Alexander Hooper, "The Negro and the Fourteenth Amendment," *Harper's Magazine,* XLVIII (1904), 438.

53 *Ibid.*

54 Message of Governor James K. Vardaman to the Mississippi Legislature, January 9, 1909, as quoted in Horace M. Bond, *The Education of the Negro in the American Social Order* (New York, 1934), 102. Charles F. Adams, "Reflex Light From Africa," *Century Magazine,* LXXII (1906), 107, declared that: "The Negro, after emancipation, should have been dealt with not as a political equal [but] . . . as a ward and dependent."

55 Woodson, *loc. cit.,* 10.

56 *Ibid.,* 53.

only six were decided in favor of the Negro petitioner.[57] Indeed, the amendment was invoked more frequently and more successfully to protect corporate wealth against state activity [58] than to protect Negroes in their constitutional rights. One authority, writing in 1911, observed that the operation of the Fourteenth Amendment had resulted in no positive gain to the Negro.[59]

One cause of the dearth of cases involving the Negro and the Fourteenth Amendment during the period prior to 1920 was the fact that the Supreme Court's conservative construction and narrow application of the amendment tended to discourage litigation. Many who might feel aggrieved would hesitate to invoke the amendment because of the feeling that the final decision would be unsatisfactory. Moreover, jurisdiction of the Supreme Court could sometimes be gained only after years of litigation. This was prohibitive in itself as far as most Negroes were concerned because of the expense involved. Moreover, when the case did finally reach the Supreme Court for decision, observed one writer:

> If in the long process he [the Negro] failed to observe all of the technical rules of legal procedure which went with the enforcement of a constitutional right in the Federal courts, his case would be dismissed.[60]

These factors generally discouraged Negroes from seeking the protection which the Fourteenth Amendment was designed to give. Seldom were they even able to exhaust the available corrective processes in the state; and this was necessary before relief could be successfully sought in Federal courts.[61]

---

[57] Ackiss, *loc. cit.*, 69; Collins, *op. cit.*, 68. For an analysis of these cases see Collins, *op. cit.*, 48–62.

[58] Edward T. Lee, "Should Not the Fourteenth Amendment to the Constitution of the United States Be Amended?", 42 *Commercial Law Review* 70, 71, suggests amending the Fourteenth Amendment so that it will apply only to "natural persons" and thus exclude corporations from its protection.

[59] Charles W. Collins, "The Fourteenth Amendment and the Negro Race Question," 45 *American Law Review* 853.

[60] Charles W. Collins, *The Fourteenth Amendment and the States*, 23.

[61] Fred Minnis, "The Attitude of Federal Courts Toward the Exclusion of Negroes from Jury Service," unpublished master's thesis, Howard University, 1934, 41.

Long before 1920, the Fourteenth Amendment had ceased to exist as a guarantee of protection for the Negro against social discrimination and political inequality. Judicial interpretation and application had so effectively stripped the amendment of its basic guarantees that efforts to enforce it registered no positive gains for the Negro.[62] No permanent results followed the infrequent attempts at Federal intervention in the Negro's behalf under authority of the Fourteenth Amendment. Moreover, Negroes were neither sufficiently organized nor sufficiently vocal to gain for themselves the guarantees which the amendment embodied.

---

[62] Charles W. Collins, "The Fourteenth Amendment and the Negro Race Question," 45 *American Law Review* 853, 854.

CHAPTER II

FOLLOWING OLD PATHS, 1920–1930

In fundamental social changes, which commonly follow national crises and important national developments, there are sometimes found the causes of extended legal controversy. Periods of warfare so disturb the national fabric that new problems in a new range of social relationships are the heritage in the post-war era. All too often, controversies arising from difficulties inherent in these relationships are solved only after a resort to the courts.

In no instance is this more the case than in regard to the Negro in the decade immediately following the World War. Entirely new social relationships and social attitudes were the Negro's heritage from the World War: his place of abode was changed; his manner of making a living was vastly different from that of pre-war years; his desire to participate in larger measure in American society tended to mount. Such changes necessitated an adjustment which would be neither rapid nor easy; for it involved new relationships with whites in sections of the country where the social pattern, as it concerned Negroes, had been firmly cast many years before. Consequently, there was an appeal to the courts by Negroes to force the adjustment under constitutional sanction and by whites to withstand it on the same basis. Most frequently invoked by the Negro for this purpose was the equal protection clause of the Fourteenth Amendment. Eighteen cases in all, which involved the Negro and the Fourteenth Amendment, were decided by American courts during the decade 1920–1930; and most of these cases were decided under the equal protection clause.

The sociological factors which were responsible for most of the litigation under the Fourteenth Amendment by Negroes during this period were either the product of, or inextricably connected with, the "Negro Migration"—a population movement of the twenties which tended to work a new areal distribution of the Negro population in the United States. In response to industrial and economic demands, the American Negro population became noticeably mobile during the World War;[1] and it remained increasingly so during the first four years of the twenties. The migration appeared to reach its height in 1924;[2] however, the migratory tendency which appeared during the early years of the decade continued to be evident, though on a much smaller scale, even in the worst years of the depression.[3]

The movement of the Negro population assumed a twofold aspect: there was a tendency to migrate from southern to northern areas, and there was also the tendency to migrate from rural to urban areas. This latter tendency, the movement to industrial and commercial centers, was especially significant even where the migration was entirely intrasectional,[4] for it resulted in a phenomenal increase in the Negro population of most southern cities and tended to increase the strain on racial relationships in these areas.

The mass movement of Negroes between 1920 and 1930, especially the South-North movement, has been attributed to various factors. These have been designated as economic, social, and socio-psychological in nature.[5] The operation of all three of these factors is well illustrated in the enlightening statement of a Negro attorney of Richmond, Virginia, who saw three groups

---

[1] George E. Haynes, *The Negro Migration and Its Implication North and South* (New York, 1923), 2–4, supports the thesis that the migration was merely an acceleration of a tendency which had been evident and which had been going on since 1865. See also "Economic Causes of the Negro Exodus," *Literary Digest,* LXXVIII (1923), 14 f.

[2] Every issue of *Opportunity: A Journal of Negro Life* (hereafter cited as *Opportunity*) for 1924 carried either an article or an editorial on some aspect of the migration. "The Northern Movement of Negroes seems to be gaining impetus," observed a Negro editor in 1923. *Opportunity,* I (1923), 28.

[3] Gunnar Myrdal, *An American Dilemma* (New York, 1944), I, 196 f.

[4] Haynes, *op. cit.,* 4.

[5] Louise V. Kennedy, *The Negro Peasant Turns Cityward* (New York, 1930), 41–58; H. Snyder, "Negro Migration and the Cotton Crop," *North American Review,* CCXIX (1924), 21–29; P. O. Davis, "Negro Exodus and Southern Agriculture," *Review of Reviews,* LXVIII (1923), 401–07.

of Negroes leaving the South: one group was leaving because of a fear of being lynched; another because of the feeling that more money could be earned in the North; and another because of the desire to obtain proper educational facilities for their children.[6] There was evidence of "unrest among colored people in the South," observed a witness before a Senate Subcommittee in 1924, "and every colored man who can get away from there is leaving as fast as he can."[7]

Economic conditions appear to have been among the most prominent reasons for the exodus. Negro leaders of Georgia were especially concerned over the low wages paid for farm labor, bad working conditions on plantations, and the general lack of credit facilities for Negro farmers.[8] Southern agriculture was undergoing a transition in this period which tended to accentuate these problems. On the other hand, industrial expansion, greatly increased by war-stimulation and continuing into the post-war years, when coupled with restrictions on immigration, created a demand for Negro labor in the northern labor market.

Some contemporaries attributed the migration to race friction, injustice, and fears of persecution in the South. Joseph H. Stewart, a Negro attorney of Washington, D. C., declared that the entire trouble was "the Laws are not executed as they are printed in the Constitution and the Statutes."[9] At a convention of Negro Republicans in Mississippi, some alarm was expressed over the unfair application of laws and mob violence.[10] One investigator has attempted to show that the exodus was greatest from those counties which had been the scene of the largest

---

[6] Statement of Giles B. Jackson before the Senate Committee on the Judiciary, Subcommittee, *Hearing on the Creation of a Commission on the Race Question,* May 24, 1924 (Washington, D. C., 1924), 11.

[7] *Ibid.,* 2–4, testimony of Dr. Jesse Lawson, President of the National Sociological Society. See Snyder, *loc. cit.,* 23–29.

[8] *Negro Year-Book,* 1925–1926 (Tuskegee, Ala., 1927), 7. Donald H. Henderson, *Urbanization of the American Negro* (New Haven, 1937), 190.

[9] U. S. Senate Committee on the Judiciary, *op. cit.,* 17, a statement made before the Committee.

[10] *Negro Year-Book,* 1923–1924, 9.

number of lynchings.[11] However, despite the existence of conditions in some areas that would seem to justify such fears, it appears that Negroes who left the South were motivated "more by the desire to improve their economic status than by fear of being manhandled by unfriendly whites." [12] The latter explanation was probably a more sentimental explanation, but it appears not entirely true. This conclusion is further supported by the fact that many Negroes, who were on the move, were drawn to urban areas of the South by the rapid industrial development of certain southern cities and thus remained in the section.[13]

The full extent of the Negro migration is realized only when population statistics of 1920 and 1930 are compared. During this decade, there was an increase in the percentage of Negroes in the total population in all of the northern geographical divisions. The largest increases, from 600,183 or 2.7 per cent in 1920 to 1,052,830 or 4 per cent in 1930 and 514,554 or 2.4 per cent to 930,450 or 3.7 per cent, were registered in the middle Atlantic States and the East North Central States respectively.[14] Michigan, Indiana, Illinois, New York, and New Jersey had a percentage increase in their Negro populations of 1.5 per cent or more, while percentage decreases ranging from 6.2 per cent to 3.1 per cent were registered in South Carolina, Georgia, Florida, and Virginia during the decade 1920–1930.[15] Much of the increase took place during the first four years of the decade; nevertheless, the tendency toward an increase in the percentage of Negroes in the total population remained a demographic characteristic of the northern geographical sections throughout the decade.

---

[11] Oswald G. Villard, "The Crumbling Color Line," *Harper's Magazine,* CLIX (1931), 158.

[12] Charles S. Johnson, "How Much is the Migration a Flight from Persecution?", *Opportunity* I (1923), 272. Donald Young, *American Minority Peoples* (New York, 1932), 43–49, finds a decrease in lynchings in the South during the late twenties and a trend toward improved race relations.

[13] Henderson, *op. cit.,* 190.

[14] United States Bureau of the Census, Fifteenth Census of the United States, *Population* (Washington, D. C., 1933), II, 38; also *Abstract of the Fourteenth Census,* 1920 (Washington, D. C., 1923), 98.

[15] *Ibid.*

Negro migrants showed a marked preference for the large cities of the North and Mid-West. Among these cities, all over 100,000 in population, were Cincinnati, Detroit, Cleveland, and Philadelphia, all of which increased the percentage of their Negro population to the total population by more than three per cent.[16] Two different attitudes toward the exodus of Negroes were expressed by southerners. One group feared a disastrous result on southern agriculture and urged "a changed public opinion [in regard to the Negro] and demonstrations of this changed public opinion" in order "to secure for the Negro a square deal." Money was raised to organize and carry out such a program. In some instances statutory means were employed to stop the migration. A second group felt that "in the long run and in the broad view only good can come from the continuance of the movement."[17] It would thin out the Negro population and constitute a solution of the Negro problem for the South.

There was an increase in the Negro population of most southern cities, corresponding in some measure with that taking place in northern cities; however, this increase was on a much smaller scale.[18] Even southern cities offered attractions to the Negro migrant which the countryside lacked. Between 1920 and 1930 the number of urban Negroes in the United States increased from 3,559,473 to 5,193,913.[19] The tendency toward urbanization was evidenced in the states of the deep-South and border region, as well as in those of the North. Substantial increases in the urban Negro population were registered in these states.[20]

The wholesale movement of Negroes into urban areas in the twenties necessitated fundamental readjustments on the part of both Negroes and the communities into which they entered. In

---

16 *Ibid.*, II, 67–73. See also Henderson, *op. cit.*, 186.

17 "Is the Black-Belt Fading?", *Literary Digest*, LXXII (Feb. 15, 1922), 23 f. For a detailed treatment of these attitudes, see New York *Times*, January 20, 1924, 16; Leo Alilunas, "Statutory Means of Impeding the Emigration of Negroes," *Journal of Negro History*, XXII (1937), 148–62.

18 Thomas J. Woofter, *Negro Problems in Cities* (New York, 1928), 26; Henderson, *op. cit.*, 188.

19 United States Bureau of the Census, *op. cit.*, II, 34.

20 *Ibid.*, 60–65.

some instances the process of urbanization was made the more difficult by the racial friction which the movement generated. The situation resulted in the ultimate appeal by Negroes to the Fourteenth Amendment and the courts for protection against the actions of whites which they interpreted as trespasses upon their rights of citizenship.

Residential Segregation: Ordinance and Covenant

The attempt to restrict residences of Negroes to certain sections of the city was the first and most obvious result of the trek of Negroes to urban areas. Such a tendency usually appeared in any city to which Negroes went in large numbers. Bad housing was one of the problems which confronted Negroes in most cities. Economic and social factors forced them to concentrate in sections of the city which were in a stage of transition from residential to commercial zones and where housing was decidedly inadequate, unsanitary, and overcrowded.[21] Available housing for Negroes tended to increase less rapidly than the demand which was continuously stimulated by the growth in the Negro population of the city. One group which studied the urban Negro problem concluded that: "The scarcity of available houses for Negroes, and the high rates charged for such as could be purchased or rented constituted the Negroes' chief problem." [22]

Expansion of the Negro residential area was necessary; and yet expansion was impeded by racial considerations. Racial attitudes of the community favored the segregation of Negroes in certain sections of the city and opposed expansion regardless of the need for more available housing or the improved economic status of Negroes who would be most affected. One writer has observed that while housing troubles were not peculiar to the Negro, his:

---

[21] For an extensive treatment of Negro housing in urban areas during this period see Woofter, *op. cit.*, 40–67; "Exploitation That is Getting Dangerous," *World Outlook,* V (1919), 14, 38; Charles S. Johnson, *The Negro in American Civilization* (New York, 1930), 207–11.

[22] President's Conference on Home Ownership and Home-Building, *Report of the Committee on Negro Housing* (Washington, D. C., 1932), 11.

> . . . situation is more complex and serious because of the emotional tension involved and the race prejudice of the white people who discourage attempts of the Negroes to expand or change their customary residential area.[23]

White residents generally opposed the expansion of Negro residential areas, for such expansion would bring Negro residents into white neighborhoods.

Demands for residential segregation were inspired by both racial and financial considerations. Many whites did not desire Negroes for neighbors; racial attitudes made them unwelcome in white communities. Proximity meant undesirable contacts, suggestions of social equality, and resultant racial antagonism.[24] Financial reasons for residential segregation were founded upon the conviction that the presence of Negroes lessened property values.[25] Whites, who would otherwise be interested in purchasing property, would not do so if Negroes lived close by. A wave of hysteria seized property owners when the first Negro moved into an area, and property was sold with little regard for its value.

The movement for residential segregation was described by one sociologist as:

> . . . only one case among many of the workings of the process of segregation in the sorting and sifting of the different elements in the growth of the city.[26]

Residential segregation assumed new importance in the twenties. Most communities failed to realize that the expansion of Negro

---

23 Kennedy, *op. cit.*, 143.

24 Arthur T. Martin, "The Segregation of Residences of Negroes," 32 *Michigan Law Review*, 723.

25 Investigators have demonstrated that property depreciation attributed to Negro residence is often the result of other factors, largely economic factors, which were generally overlooked, and that sections into which Negroes expanded were areas in which property values were already declining. Editorial, *Crisis*, XXXI (1925), 9; Kennedy, *op. cit.*, 149 f.; President's Conference on Home Ownership and Home Building, *op. cit.*, 19–22.

26 Ernest W. Burgess, "Residential Segregation in American Cities," in *The American Negro, Annals of the American Academy of Political and Social Science*, CXL (1928), 105.

residential areas was a natural sociological process which should have been provided for by town-planning. While the movement was most obvious in Washington, D. C., and cities of the border and southern states, where the ideal of complete segregation in housing had become crystallized, northern cities revealed a mounting interest in accomplishing the same end. Here the practice had been quietly carried on for years.[27]

Earliest attempts to effect residential segregation made use of the legislative process. Beginning in 1910, cities of the South and border states adopted segregation ordinances. Baltimore, Maryland, took the lead in 1910 and was soon followed by other cities.[28] The purpose of such legislation, as generally stated in the ordinance, was "to prevent conflict and ill-feeling between the white and colored races and to preserve the public peace and promote the general welfare."[29] To this might be added the unexpressed intent of protecting property values. State police powers were called upon to support such enactments. There was a great deal of similarity in all of the ordinances. They either restricted the residence of whites in all-Negro blocks and Negroes in all-white blocks; divided the city into segregated districts and designated a district for each race; or restricted new residences in mixed blocks to the racial group which had established a majority of the residences in the block.[30]

These municipal ordinances, supported by small property owners, real estate dealers, and petty politicians, were generally upheld in courts of last resort in the states as an appropriate

---

27 Hannibal C. Duncan, *The Changing Race Relationship in the Border and Northern States* (Phil., Pa., 1922), 25; Kennedy, *op. cit.*, 144–46; N.A.A.C.P., *Fifteenth Annual Report,* 1924, 21–22; Paul E. Baker, *Negro-White Adjustment* (Pittsfield, Mass., 1924), 120–24.

28 Winston Salem, North Carolina, 1912; Madisonville, Kentucky, 1913; Birmingham, Alabama, 1913; Atlanta, Georgia, 1913; Richmond, Virginia, 1913; Norfolk, Virginia, 1913; Louisville, Kentucky, 1915; St. Louis, Missouri, 1916; Dallas, Texas, 1916.

29 See *Buchanan v. Warley,* 245 U. S. 60 (1917).

30 For a detailed treatment of various types of segregation ordinances see Thomas J. Woofter, *Negro Problems in Cities,* 69–71. Duncan, *op. cit.,* 23, treats the unsuccessful effort to extend segregation legislation to the rural areas of North Carolina.

exercise of state police powers and, therefore, were not prohibited by the Fourteenth Amendment. The Supreme Court ruling in the case of *Buchanan v. Warley*,[31] invalidating the Louisville, Kentucky ordinance, made it difficult to construct segregation ordinances which would stand the constitutional test of "due process of law." However, between 1920 and 1929, several cities made the attempt.

A segregation ordinance, similar in many respects to that of Louisville, Kentucky, which had been declared unconstitutional by the Supreme Court in 1917, was enacted in Norfolk, Virginia, in August, 1925. The local branch of the National Association for the Advancement of Colored People contested the ordinance in the courts of Virginia, and it was declared an unconstitutional exercise of state police power.[32]

Indianapolis enacted an ordinance, on May 16, 1926, which limited districts of the city in which Negroes might establish residences and forbade the residence of whites in Negro districts.[33] In November, 1926, the Marrow County Circuit Court ruled the ordinance a violation of the Fourteenth Amendment under the rule laid down in the case of *Buchanan v. Warley*.[34]

Segregation ordinances enacted by New Orleans, Richmond, and Dallas resulted in three significant cases between 1927–1929. All three of the ordinances were designed in an effort to circumvent the rule of *Buchanan v. Warley*. The New Orleans ordinance, enacted under authority of an empowering state statute in 1924, forbade the establishment of a residence by a white person in a Negro community or by a Negro in a white community "without the written consent of a majority of the persons of the opposite race in the community affected." Such consent must be filed with the Mayor of the city. Each seven days' residence, in violation of these provisions, constituted a separate offense and might be criminally punished.[35]

Negroes, as well as whites who owned property which they

---

[31] 245 U. S. 60.

[32] N.A.A.C.P., *Seventeenth Annual Report*, 1926, 10.

[33] New York *Times*, March 17, 1926, 3.

[34] *Negro Year-Book*, 1931–1932, 68.

[35] *Tyler v. Harmon*, 104 So. 200, 201 (La., 1925).

desired to sell to Negroes, became alarmed and expressed dissatisfaction over the ordinance. From the Negro's point of view, the ordinance in question was an attempt to create Negro ghettos "by confining them to deteriorated areas." [36] Such action, they felt, both violated their rights of citizenship and was conducive to intensified race friction.

The New Orleans ordinance came before the courts in 1924 when Tyler, who owned property in a "white community," sought an injunction in the Civil District Court of Louisiana to restrain Harmon, who owned a cottage opposite him, from renting the same to Negro tenants. Tyler claimed the written consent of a majority of white residents had not been obtained as provided by law. It was contended that Harmon's intended action was aimed at the violation of the city ordinance.[37] As the litigation began, the Director of Branches of the National Association for the Advancement of Colored People, who was in New Orleans, wrote:

> It is expected that the desire for re-election and approval of their white constituency will cause the judges in the Civil Courts, the Court of Appeals, and the State Supreme Court to give adverse decisions even though it is clear that the United States Supreme Court has already . . . declared this act unconstitutional. It is felt that the judge would prefer to be reversed rather than be subject to the criticism of having rendered a decision in favor of the Negro.[38]

If this observation was accurate, the issue of constitutionality was destined to be finally settled in the United States Supreme Court; for there was the latent possibility that if this ordinance was upheld, other cities would be encouraged to enact similar measures.

Harmon urged the unconstitutionality of the ordinance before the local court on the grounds that its enforcement would constitute a violation of the "due process of law" clause of the

---

[36] Madge Headley, "Citizen Rights and Community Rights," *Opportunity,* I (1923), 12–14; Duncan, *op. cit.,* 29.

[37] *Tyler v. Harmon,* 104 So. 200.

[38] Letter of Robert N. Bagwell to the National Office, November, 1924, quoted in *Crisis,* XXIX (1924), 20.

Fourteenth Amendment. Contrary to expectations, the plea was upheld and the prayer for an injunction was dismissed. However, on Tyler's appeal, the Supreme Court of Louisiana reversed the decision. It was held that no discrimination of any sort against either race would result from the operation of the contested ordinance, for "the rights which are denied to each race are the same." Moreover, the restriction of residence was a matter of "social distinction, not political or civil rights," and was not violative of the Fourteenth Amendment.[39]

The case was carried to the United States Supreme Court by Harmon on appeal. He argued that the decision handed down by the Supreme Court of Louisiana violated the rule of *Buchanan v. Warley*. Counsel for Louisiana contended that the rule, which was relied upon by the appellant, should be modified in response to the vast changes which had taken place during the years since the rule was announced. Furthermore, the problem of residential segregation was no longer a southern problem; it was a problem which concerned northern cities as well.[40] The argument failed to move the Court. In a *per curiam* decision, which applied the rule of *Buchanan v. Warley,* the decision of the Supreme Court of Louisiana was reversed, and the ordinance was declared unconstitutional.[41]

It appears that reversal was not entirely unexpected "in view of the attitude of the Supreme Court in matters of this kind in the past." [42] However, there was disappointment in that the decision left New Orleans "without any legal method of restricting Negro residents to any particular residential section." [43]

A unique segregation ordinance was enacted by the Board of Aldermen of Richmond, Virginia, on February 15, 1929.[44] It

---

[39] *Tyler v. Harmon,* 104 So. 202, 205.

[40] New York *Times,* March 15, 1927, 12; New Orleans *Times-Picayune,* March 15, 1927, 1–2.

[41] *Harmon v. Tyler,* 273 U. S. 668 (1927). A *per curiam* decision is one in which all the judges agree and in which an elaborate or extended decision is deemed unnecessary. A *per curiam* decision has as much weight and authority as any other form of decision.

[42] New Orleans *States,* March 14, 1927, 1.

[43] *Ibid.*

[44] A telegram from the National Office of the National Association for

attempted to evade the rule laid down by the Supreme Court in matters of this kind by forbidding residence in the same block of those persons who were forbidden by law to intermarry. By framing the ordinance in this way, the ban against intermarriage rather than color was the basis of restriction. A Negro, J. B. Deans, brought action to enjoin enforcement of the ordinance claiming that its operation would contravene the Fourteenth Amendment. The United States District Court in Richmond declared the ordinance invalid.[45] The city of Richmond appealed to the United States Circuit Court, urging that since the restriction was based upon the legal prohibition of intermarriage rather than color, it did not trespass upon any of the guarantees of the Fourteenth Amendment. Despite this fine and forced distinction, the Circuit Court could find no essential difference between this ordinance and those which had already been declared invalid in the cases of *Buchanan v. Warley* and *Harmon v. Tyler.* The court declared: "As the legal prohibition of intermarriage is itself based on race, the question here, in the final analysis, is identical with that which the Supreme Court has twice decided [adversely] in the cases cited."[46] Therefore, the lower court was upheld. Ultimate appeal to the United States Supreme Court resulted in the reaffirmation of the rule that residential segregation, by legislative action, violated the "due process" clause of the Fourteenth Amendment.[47]

Dallas, Texas, also attempted to by-pass the Supreme Court's proscription against segregation ordinances. Acting under authority of a state statute, the city government passed an ordi-

---

the Advancement of Colored People urged the Mayor of Richmond to veto the ordinance on the basis of the rules already established by the Supreme Court in such matters. He refused to take this action saying: "Those who oppose it are entirely within their rights in having the courts pass upon its constitutionality." *Crisis,* XXXVI (1929), 121. An identical ordinance was enacted in Atlanta, Georgia, on May 20, 1929. See *Negro Year-Book,* 1931–1932, 67.

[45] *City of Richmond v. Deans,* 37 Fed. (2d) 712 (C.C.A. 4th Ct., 1930).

[46] *Ibid.,* 713. Cases referred to were *Buchanan v. Warley* and *Harmon v. Tyler.*

[47] *City of Richmond v. Deans,* 281 U. S. 704 (1930). A *per curiam* decision.

nance on December 15, 1927, requiring the observance of agreements entered into by white and Negro residents in respect to areas of the city which each race would inhabit.[48] Residence in an area in disregard of such agreements constituted a criminal offense.

The Liberty Annex Corporation, a real estate concern which was interested in selling lots in a restricted area to Negroes, contested the ordinance. Though the ordinance was based upon a voluntary agreement, freely entered into by the signatory parties, the courts of Texas found no difficulty in pronouncing the ordinance unconstitutional because it constituted a trespass upon the guarantees of the Fourteenth Amendment. The Court reasoned that the segregation agreement was valid as between the signatory parties; however, in punishing, criminally, breaches of the agreement, the municipality had exceeded its police powers. "The right to occupy," concluded the opinion, "may not be denied solely on the basis of color without a denial of due process of law."[49] The ordinance was declared invalid. So firmly was the rule against residential segregation by legislative action established by 1930 that, since that time, contested ordinances of this sort have generally been invalidated in courts of first instance.[50]

All efforts to effect residential segregation by municipal action under state authority during this period failed. The courts consistently applied the "due process" clause and found such action, based on color, denied a constitutional right guaranteed by the Fourteenth Amendment, the right to use and to dispose of property. Much adverse criticism appeared in response to this application of the amendment. Such an application was termed "judicial solicitude for property rights" and an attempt by the Federal government to establish social equality between the races.[51] Despite the constitutional view on this question, as re-

[48] *Liberty Annex Corporation v. City of Dallas,* 289 S. W. 1067 (Court of Civil Appeals, Tex., 1927).

[49] *Ibid.,* 1068; also *City of Dallas v. Liberty Annex Corporation,* 19 S.W. (2d) 846 (Court of Civil Appeals, Tex., 1929).

[50] New York *Times,* February 14, 1931, 18; *Negro Year-Book,* 1931–1932, 67.

[51] Andrew C. Bruce, "Racial Zoning by Private Contract," 26 *Illinois Law Review* 708.

flected by the courts, there persisted a strong popular sentiment favorable to the enactment of such ordinances.[52] In the opinion of one authority, it appeared that the failure of ordinances to fix residential boundaries by law was due "more to the inescapable wording of the Constitution than to the choice of the active element of the . . . population."[53]

With the failure of segregation ordinances, land covenants were adopted to accomplish the same purpose which had been attempted with ordinances. These covenants were property agreements, running with the land, whereby the signatories agreed neither to sell nor to permit the occupancy of their property by persons of African descent for a stipulated period of time.[54] Property agreements of this character have been viewed as "a social expansion of the principle of zoning" in which segregation ordinances are written into deeds of land and residence.[55]

Property agreements possessed qualities which made them effective instruments in circumventing the constitutional difficulties which segregation ordinances had encountered. Most important of all was the fact that they were the product of individual rather than state action; they would, therefore, appear to be beyond the scope of the Fourteenth Amendment according to the doctrine established in the *Civil Rights* cases. Commenting on the effectiveness of restrictive covenants, one writer observed: "The decisions of the Supreme Court had no appreciable effect . . . the process [of segregation] goes on as effectively without the law as with it."[56] Here was an instrument which could prevent

[52] Major Gardner, "Racial Segregation in Cities," 29 *Kentucky Law Journal,* 216, 219; Arthur J. Martin, *loc. cit.,* 721; John J. Jones, *The Negroes Are an Economic Problem* (Jamaica, New York, 1933), 141–59.

[53] President's Conference on Home Ownership and Home Building, *op. cit.,* 40.

[54] See Lewis R. Donelson, "The Enforceability of Restrictive Covenants on Lands in the District of Columbia," 29 *Georgetown Law Journal,* 500, 508, for a discussion of early uses of land covenants.

[55] Charles S. Johnson, *Patterns of Negro Segregation* (New York, 1943), 177. See also James W. Johnson, "Legal Aspects of the Negro Problem," in *Annals of the American Academy of Political and Social Science,* CXL (1928), 93.

[56] Kelly Miller and Herbert Seligmann, "Separate Communities for Negroes," *Current History,* XXV (1927), 827.

Negroes from residing in exclusively white residential areas; and there was every prospect that the courts would enforce such agreements.

Perhaps the earliest decision on restrictive covenants, designed to segregate on a racial basis, was that in the case of *Gandolpho v. Hartman,*[57] decided in the United States Circuit Court for California in 1892. In this instance supporters of the covenant in question held that it was the product of individual action, not state action, and that it was not within the inhibitions of the Fourteenth Amendment. Nevertheless, the court disallowed this interpretation and ruled the covenant a violation of the Fourteenth Amendment. The opinion said in part: "Any result inhibited by the Constitution can no more be accomplished by contract of individual citizens than by legislation, and the Courts shall no more enforce the one than the other." [58]

No attempt was made to have the United States Supreme Court rule on the constitutionality of restrictive covenants between 1892–1926. Meanwhile, the courts of last resort in the states generally upheld them as enforceable in equity and beyond the protective scope of the Fourteenth Amendment.[59] Between 1920 and 1926, conditions became such that some interested groups urged a Supreme Court ruling on the question of the constitutionality of restrictive covenants under the Fourteenth Amendment. The rapid migration of Negroes to cities and the ruling that segregation under legislative enactment was unconstitutional led to wider usage of restrictive covenants to effect racial segregation in cities of the South and border states. St. Louis real estate dealers, alarmed at the annual addition of 30,000 Negroes to the population of that city, established "Negro Zones" by private contract.[60] Other cities, particularly Washington, D. C., followed the example; and the "disturbing question of Negro residence

---

57 49 Fed. 181.

58 *Ibid.*

59 *Parmalee v. Morris,* 188 N.W. 330 (Mich., 1922); *Title Guarantee and Trust Company v. Garrot,* 183 Pac. 470 (Calif., 1919); and cases therein cited.

60 George W. Buckner, "St. Louis Revives the Segregation Issue," *Opportunity,* I (1923), 238.

areas" concerned more than twenty large cities in five different states and the District of Columbia before 1926.[61]

The acuteness of the problem in Washington, D. C., resulted in court litigation and the controlling decision in the case of *Corrigan v. Buckley.*[62] In 1921 thirty white persons, including Irene Corrigan, entered into an agreement whereby each agreed not to sell or lease his property to any person of Negro blood for a period of twenty-one years. However, the following year Corrigan contracted to sell her property to Helen Curtis, a person of Negro blood. Buckley, one of the covenanters, sued to enjoin conveyance of the property in violation of the contractual agreement. Curtis asked dismissal of the suit for enforcement on the claim that it would work a denial of equal protection of the law as guaranteed by the Fourteenth Amendment. This contention was disallowed and the parties were enjoined. The decision was affirmed by the Court of Appeals of the District of Columbia, and the United States Supreme Court agreed to review the case on the claim of the defendant that it involved the construction and application of the Constitution of the United States.[63]

Nation-wide interest was manifest in the case, for on its outcome depended the fate of similar covenants in other jurisdictions. The significance of the impending decision was fully appreciated; and since the failure of segregation ordinances, it would finally determine whether or not there was any instrument under which residential segregation could be legally enforced. One Negro leader remarked: "The entire question of residential segregation in America will be determined by the Court's decision," for the case involved:

> . . . The question of residential segregation, not only against colored people in America, but against Catholics, Jews, and any other group property owners may care to bar out by agreement among themselves. . . . If this color bar against colored people is sustained it will have the practical effect of nullifying . . . the Louisville

[61] Editorial, *Opportunity,* IV (1926), 336; Louise V. Kennedy, *The Negro Peasant Turns Cityward,* 148; New York *Times,* November 1, 1925, IX, 15.

[62] 271 U. S. 323 (1926).

[63] *Corrigan v. Buckley,* 299 Fed. 898 (1924); 271 U. S. 328.

> Case. . . . It would mean more crowding in colored residential districts, more exploitation of colored tenants, besides a legal sanction for a slur upon colored Americans. . . .[64]

The New York *Times* tersely stated: "The decision in the Buckley case will severely affect the residential status of colored Americans and all other minority groups throughout the United States."[65] Groups of white property owners in the District of Columbia, realizing the importance of the case in the final determination of the question of the enforceability of restrictive covenants, collected more than $1,000.00 to help finance the case. On the other side, the Negro interest was aided by the National Association for the Advancement of Colored People which furnished legal counsel.[66]

The decision was handed down five months after the petition for review was granted, and it was read by Mr. Justice Sanford. The position of the Court was indicated in the first part of the decision when it was cautioned that:

> The mere assertion that the case is one involving the construction or application of the Constitution, and in which the construction of federal laws is drawn into question, does not, however, authorize this Court to entertain the appeal; and it is our duty to decline jurisdiction if the record does not present such a constitutional or statutory question, substantial in character and properly raised below.[67]

Justice Sanford first refuted the contention of the petitioner that since the legislative power was forbidden to enact segregation legislation, compulsive enforcement of covenants in equity would

---

[64] Statement of Attorney James A. Cobb. *Crisis,* XXIX (1924), 19 f. The question of residential segregation in regard to Chinese and Mexicans had been raised more than two decades before in California and Texas.

[65] November 1, 1925, IX, 15.

[66] Editorial comment, "The Washington Segregation Case," *Crisis,* XXIX (1924), 69.

[67] 271 U. S. 329. Justice Sanford had been on the Court three years when he read this opinion. He was born and educated in Tennessee where he also served as federal judge for several years.

work a denial of due process of law which was equally forbidden to the judicial authority. "It is State action of a particular character that is forbidden," reasoned Justice Sanford; "individual invasion of individual rights is not the subject-matter of the Amendment." [68] An examination of the record revealed that neither the Fourteenth Amendment, nor statutes enacted in aid and under its authority, prohibited or invalidated contracts entered into by private individuals in respect to the control and disposition of their property. The opinion continued: "We therefore conclude that neither the Constitution nor statutory questions relied on as ground for the appeal to this Court have any substantial quality or color of merit, or afford any jurisdictional basis for the appeal." [69] Moreover, the contention that the enforcement of the decrees of the court below, in themselves, worked a deprivation of liberty and property without due process of law, the Court would not consider; for the petitioner had failed to raise the question in the petition for appeal, or by assignment of error.[70] Therefore, the contention could not serve as a jurisdictional basis for the appeal. The case was dismissed for want of jurisdiction.

Many and varied were the reactions to the decision. Some persons felt that the Court had purposely evaded the issue. The Court "wisely exercised the precaution of disclaiming away the purpose of passing on the fundamental question because of lack of jurisdiction," commented the President of the National Association for the Advancement of Colored People.[71] However, viewing residential segregation as the foremost issue facing the race, the Association began making plans to bring the issue before the Court "so unequivocally that a decision cannot be avoided." [72] Others expressed the belief that the decision settled forever the question of the right of persons to develop property and to place

---

68 *Ibid.*, 331.

69 *Ibid.*

70 *Ibid.*

71 Statement of Attorney Moorfield Storey. *Crisis,* XXXII (1926), 115.

72 Statement of Walter White, Assistant Secretary of the National Association for the Advancement of Colored People. *Opportunity,* IV (1926), 239. See also New York *Times,* June 1, 1926, 8.

racial restrictions upon it;[73] it was but a recognition that whites have property rights which should be protected when they are threatened with conditions which would destroy their value.[74] To those who were unsympathetic toward residential segregation through restrictive covenants, it appeared certain that the decision would stimulate action to bar Negroes and "other undesirable groups" from certain communities.[75]

The decision in *Corrigan v. Buckley* remained the controlling decision in subsequent cases which invoked the Fourteenth Amendment against restrictive covenants. The problem of residential segregation was to be controlled through individual action in the absence of state competency to do so through legislative action. It does appear that the latter method would be preferable and would have the merit of orderly, systematic planning, if residential segregation of a non-voluntary nature was to be a fact; however, the construction of the Fourteenth Amendment, as applied by the Supreme Court since 1883, precluded this.

Negro Disfranchisement

The problem of Negro disfranchisement in southern states concerned many Negro leaders during the twenties. To disfranchisement was attributed much of the injustice and inequality which Negroes experienced in the South. Disfranchisement itself was considered a most glaring and unconstitutional denial of the

---

[73] Donald Young, *American Minority Peoples* (New York, 1934), 188, holds that "even if covenants as a means of insuring racial integrity were declared illegal there would possibly be little difference in the distribution of racial minorities in cities of the United States, for residential grouping . . . has gone unconcernedly ahead not only where laws and ordinances have been . . . illegally enforced but also where they have been thrown out of court, and where the legislatures have not even bothered their heads about the matter."

[74] "The Supreme Court's Jim Crow Case," *Literary Digest*, LXXIX (June 12, 1926), 14. The block which was the subject of this case was inhabited by Negroes within ten months of the decision favorable to the enforcement of the covenant. See Kelly Miller and Herbert Seligmann, "Separate Communities for Negroes," *Current History*, XXV (1927), 828.

[75] Washington *Post*, May 25, 1926, 1, 19. For a discussion of the Negro residential problem between 1940–1944, see Edwin R. Embree, *Julius Rosenwald Fund, 1942–1944* (Chicago, 1944), 4–5.

rights and privileges of American citizenship. The tendency of Negroes to concentrate in urban areas and the discriminatory conditions which they found there tended to strengthen the belief that the ballot was essential for the removal of limitations upon their rights of citizenship.

After studying the conditions surrounding the framing and adoption of the Fourteenth Amendment, it is difficult to come to any conclusion other than that Congress desired and attempted to guarantee Negro suffrage in 1868. It did so indirectly by inserting the second section into the Amendment since there was the feeling that Congress was without constitutional authority to enfranchise the Negro by direct means. This section of the amendment penalized, by reduced representation in Congress, any state which excluded the Negro from the exercise of the suffrage.[76] Fear of Negro domination in the South immediately after the Civil War, and the conviction that Negroes were corrupt politically and without the ability to perform the electoral function [77] served to stimulate a systematic exclusion of Negroes from the suffrage.[78]

Both formal and informal methods were employed to effect Negro disfranchisement; but in the main, legal forms were utilized to avoid outward conflict with the letter of the law as stated in the Fourteenth and Fifteenth Amendments.[79] Beginning in Mississippi in 1890, which was immediately followed by other southern states, disfranchisement devices were written into state constitutions and expressed in statutory form.[80]

---

76 Kirk Porter, *A History of Suffrage in the United States* (Chicago, 1918), 172–82.

77 For a criticism of this prejudiced point of view, see W. E. B. DuBois, *Black Reconstruction* (New York, 1935), 402–04, 717–27; "Mr. Beecher on Reconstruction," *Outlook,* LXXIV (1903), 286; Norman P. Andrews, "The Negro in Politics," *Journal of Negro History,* V (1920), 422.

78 Paul Lewinson, *Race, Class and Party* (New York, 1932), 46–60; Robert L. Morton, *The Negro in Virginia Politics, 1865–1902* (Charlottesvilla, Va., 1919), 144–46; William A. Mabry, *Studies in the Disfranchisement of the Negro in the South* (Durham, N. C., 1938), 173–91.

79 Gunnar Myrdal, *An American Dilemma,* I, 479–86; Lewinson, *op. cit.,* 79–81.

80 Mabry, *op. cit.,* 322–28, 176–82.

Perhaps most effective of all southern disfranchisement techniques, and from outward appearances the most legal, was the Democratic white primary. Members of the Democratic party in southern states decided that only white Democrats would be permitted to vote in the party primary. Since the outcome of the general election was always the opinion which had been expressed in the primary, the primary was, in effect, substituted for the general election in this one-party section. By excluding Negroes from the party primary, a device was found which effectively, and to all expectations legally, excluded Negroes from exercising the right of suffrage in a way which might exert any real influence upon elections in the South. Legislative sanction was obtained for the Democratic white primary in most southern states during the twenties.[81] One writer justly remarked that in the south "the center of political power is in these primaries."[82]

The conviction that the right to vote was essential to full participation in American society led Negro leaders and Negro organizations to attack the constitutionality of the white primary under the "equal protection" clause of the Fourteenth Amendment. It constituted a most effective way of striking a blow for the right to vote. An editor of a newspaper in Richmond, Virginia, commented:

> Because the exercise of their political prerogatives in general elections has no appreciable effect on political matters, southern Negroes have begun quite wisely to fight for the right to vote in the primaries. . . . And this is not a matter of empty political aspiration. . . . It is a plain case of absolute necessity.[83]

The most consistent attack of all was that made on the white primary in Texas. Here the primary was an integral part of the state election system. In 1923 a statute was enacted by the legislature which stated that in no event were Negroes eligible to

---

[81] Leo Alilunas, "Legal Restrictions on the Negro in Politics," *Journal of Negro History,*" XXV (1940), 161–80.

[82] Thomas L. Dabney, "Southern Negroes and Politics," *Opportunity,* VIII (1930), 274.

[83] *Ibid.*

vote in any Democratic party primaries in the state.[84] It appears that the measure found its inspiration in the fear that Negro Republicans, combined with a Democratic minority faction, would be able to defeat the will of the majority. The author of the statute, D. A. McAskill, had been defeated in an election in Bexar County, in 1922, by an opponent who was supported by Negroes. He sponsored the measure because he was convinced that "the Democratic party was ruined unless something was done to protect it." [85] The enactment of the law meant that that protection of the party was to come from the state, for under the statute of 1923, state sanction was given to the exclusion of Negroes from the primary. The statute was considered "a pioneer in legislation of its sort," as it was said, "nothing like it was ever attempted in Texas before, and so far as it is known, there is nothing akin to [it] in the statutes of any state." [86]

This statute of 1923 was first contested before the Federal courts in the case of *Chandler v. Neff.*[87] It arose from the action of a Negro, Hurley C. Chandler, who sought to enjoin enforcement of the law. He claimed the law contravened the "privileges and immunities" clause of the Fourteenth Amendment. However, as the Court examined the question it came to a different conclusion. It was held that the denial of the right to vote in a Democratic primary was not a right included in the words "privileges and immunities of the Constitution." Moreover, primaries were merely nominating devices and "are in no sense elections for office." Acting under its police powers, the "State may regulate primary elections and prescribe party tests." [88]

Local interests applauded the decision upholding the constitutionality of the statute. In effect it would "preserve the integrity of the Democratic party . . . throughout the State." [89] Further efforts to invalidate the measure were considered useless.

---

[84] Texas, *General Laws,* 1923, Art. 309a, 74–75.

[85] San Antonio *Express,* April 6, 1924, 3. See also Lewinson, *op. cit.,* 113.

[86] San Antonio *Express,* April 6, 1924, 3.

[87] 298 Fed. 515 (D.C.W.D. Tex., 1924).

[88] *Ibid.,* 519.

[89] San Antonio *Express,* April 6, 1924, 3; also Galveston *Daily News,* April 6, 1924, 1.

An opportunity for a ruling on the Texas statute by the United States Supreme Court presented itself in 1927 in the case of *Nixon v. Herndon.*[90] Dr. Nixon, a Negro resident of El Paso, Texas, appealed to the Court on writ of error against an adverse decision involving the Texas primary law. He contended that the measure constituted a denial of equal protection of the law as guaranteed by the Fourteenth Amendment.

Justice Holmes, who wrote the opinion, upheld Nixon's contention saying: "It is hard to imagine a more direct and obnoxious infringement of the Fourteenth" Amendment. He felt that the primary, as it operated in Texas, constituted an integral part of the state election machinery; and discrimination in a primary election, which determined the final result, was, in his opinion, an illegal discrimination. The Texas statute, despite the prohibitions of the Fourteenth Amendment, worked such a discrimination; Negroes were forbidden to participate in primaries on the distinction of color alone. "States may do a great deal of classifying that it is difficult to believe rational," he concluded, "but there are limits and it is too clear for extended argument that color cannot be made the basis of a statutory classification affecting the right set up in this case."[91] The statute was declared invalid on the ground that it effected an unconstitutional denial of equal protection of the law.

Negroes and advocates of Negro enfranchisement were generally enthusiastic over the decision. It was hailed as "a judicial landmark." Further, "it indicated what the decision of the Court must be if other trials involving discriminatory legislation against colored people are got squarely before it."[92] There was a feeling expressed that the willingness of the Court to question southern political procedure would cause something of a shock in the South and would tend to discourage discriminatory

---

[90] 273 U. S. 536.

[91] *Ibid.,* 541.

[92] New York *Times,* March 8, 1927, 24. See also the address of James W. Johnson, Secretary of the National Association for the Advancement of Colored People, before the Annual Convention of the Association in 1927. *Crisis,* XXXIV (1927), 224.

practices.[93] Justice Holmes, too, was aware of the significance of the decision. He is reported to have remarked confidentially: "I know that our good brethren, the Negroes of Texas, will now rejoice that they possess at the primary rights which heretofore they have enjoyed at the general election." [94]

It appears that the declaration of unconstitutionality was not entirely unexpected by state officials in Texas. However, they predicted that its practical effects were greatly overestimated; and as far as an increase in the number of Negro voters in Texas was concerned, its effect would be negligible.[95] The decision presented "no serious problem to the Democratic party," for plans were being made to give County Committees the power to fix qualifications for voting in party primaries.[96] Subsequent cases which attempted to force the application of the rule established in this case tend to support the position that the practical effects of the decision were overestimated.

Shortly after the adverse decision in *Nixon v. Herndon,* the legislature of Texas enacted a measure which vested authority to fix qualifications for participation in party primaries in the state executive committees of political parties. Immediately after this enactment, the State Executive Committee of the Democratic party met and established a color qualification which limited participation in the primary to white Democrats. This action was contested in the cases of *Grigsby v. Harris* [97] and *White v. Lubbock.*[98] It was contended that since the legislature of Texas had authorized state executive committees to establish a discrimination against voters, the action of the Democratic Committee was state action which violated the Fourteenth Amendment. But

---

[93] Editorial, "Nullification," *Opportunity,* V (1927), 97.

[94] George Ajootian, "The Right of Negroes to Vote in State Primaries," 12 *Boston University Law Review* 689.

[95] Galveston *Daily News,* March 8, 1927, 2. One contemporary felt that the decision was responsible for the unprecedentedly heavy registration and enrollment of Negroes in the Democratic party in western Texas. Herbert J. Seligmann, "The Negroes' Influence as a Voter," *Current History,* XXVIII (1928), 230.

[96] Houston *Post-Dispatch,* March 8, 1927, 4.

[97] 27 Fed. (2d) 942 (D.C.S.D. Tex., 1928).

[98] 30 S. W. (2d) 722 (Tex., 1930).

the court felt otherwise. It ruled that such action was "purely party action," for though parties were regulated by the state, they were not state instrumentalities. In the opinion of the court, parties had a right to decide who could participate in their primaries and conventions which was beyond statutory control.[99]

A Virginia statute, analogous in many ways to the Texas statute of 1927, had been enacted in 1924.[100] This measure established state-controlled primary elections; even primary election expenses were paid by the state. The Democratic party in Virginia had, by resolution and under authority of the primary election law, restricted participation in its primary elections to white persons. The question of unconstitutionality, no doubt inspired by the ruling in *Nixon v. Herndon,* was raised before the United States District Court in Richmond in 1928. The case arose from the fact that James C. West, a Negro resident of Richmond, Virginia, was refused a ballot to vote in a Democratic primary election by an election official. West contended that the election official had acted under authority of a state statute which had permitted the party to disqualify him; therefore, the action in refusing a ballot was state action which infringed his rights under the Fourteenth Amendment.[101] This contention is easily recognized as that advanced and supported by the Supreme Court in *Nixon v. Herndon.*

The District Court declared the contested statute in conflict with the Fourteenth Amendment. In its operation the statute had "excluded a qualified voter and adherent of the party from his right of suffrage by indirect means." This, the legislature, by virtue of the restrictions imposed by the Fourteenth Amendment, was incompetent to do either directly or indirectly; for in either instance the result was the same. "A law which recognizes or which authorizes a discriminatory test or standard," declared the court, "does curtail and subvert" constitutional rights.[102] Such an act contravened the Fourteenth Amendment.

---

[99] *Ibid.,* 724.

[100] *Virginia Code,* 1925, Ch. 15, Sec. 221, 228.

[101] *West v. Bliley et al.,* 33 Fed. (2d) 177 (1929).

[102] *Ibid.,* 180.

The court was fully aware of the importance of the decision and declared:

> That its effect [the decision's] may be to change a custom that has long obtained in the political system in this state, and therefore meet with the disapproval of many, is a consequence which, unpleasant though it may be, may nevertheless not be avoided in the performance of the duty devolving on the court.[103]

While there was considerable disapproval of the decision in Virginia, party threats to make party nominations in the state independent of state control were never effectuated. The Democratic party in Virginia appeared reluctant to assume the expenses of the primary "merely for the power to exclude Negroes from primaries."[104]

Cases before the courts during this period which involved the white primary reveal that, where race or color was adopted as a standard or test under authority of state legislation, the courts found that such a standard or test contravened the "equal protection" clause of the Fourteenth Amendment. In such instances the party failed to act as an independent association but acted as an instrumentality of the state. However, where no enabling legislation was enacted by the state, which gave state sanction to discriminatory standards established by the party, party action disqualifying Negroes from participation in party primaries, because of color, was upheld.[105] In the latter case the action was that of a voluntary political association, and as such it was beyond the scope of the Fourteenth Amendment. By 1930 party rules had been adopted by the Democratic party in eleven states of the South, which excluded Negroes from participation in party primaries; and only in two states, Texas and Virginia, could the enforcement of such rules be enjoined by invoking the guarantees of the Fourteenth Amendment.[106]

---

[103] *Ibid.*

[104] Richmond *Times-Dispatch,* June 6, 1929, 8; also issue of April 8, 1935, 8.

[105] *Robinson v. Holman,* 26 S. W. (2d) 66 (Ark., 1930).

[106] For a survey of white primary rules see G. D. Weeks, "The White Primary," 8 *Mississippi Law Journal* 140–42.

Increased urbanization on the part of the Negro population of the United States tended to focus attention upon the educational facilities provided for Negro children. Perhaps this was to be expected as the Negro population became more vocal, for Negroes had long emphasized the power of education for racial development and advancement. Racial segregation and consequent inadequate facilities, which had been effected in southern jurisdictions, appeared to be rapidly spreading into cities of the North and border states.[107] Several cases were brought before state tribunals in the twenties [108] contesting inequalities in educational facilities, as between Negro and white pupils, as a violation of the guarantees of the Fourteenth Amendment. State courts in each instance applied the "substantial equality" doctrine which was pronounced in the case of *United States v. Buntin* [109] in 1882. Equal protection of law, as it applied to education, did not demand identity in educational facilities. The United States Supreme Court affirmed this doctrine for the first time in 1927 in a case which involved the segregation of Chinese pupils in Mississippi.[110]

Interracial relations in the South have frequently been marked by violence and strife. Over a period of many decades, there had developed "a pattern of illegal practices supported by the sanction of tradition and tacitly accepted by a majority of the people" for the purpose of dealing with problems or relations involving Negroes.[111] Criminal cases involving Negroes, especially if the offense was committed against a white person, often resulted in legal action and legal practices which appeared to violate con-

---

[107] Charles S. Johnson, *Patterns of Negro Segregation,* 12.

[108] *State v. Albruther,* 224 Pac. 511 (Okla., 1924); *Greathouse v. Board of School Commissioners,* 151 N. E. 411 (Ind., 1927).

[109] *Supra,* 7.

[110] *Gong Lum v. Rice,* 275 U. S. 78. The Supreme Court held in the two cases, *Meyers v. Nebraska,* 262 U. S. 390 (1923) and *Pierce v. Society of Sisters,* 268 U. S. 510 (1925), that freedom in the selection of schools and languages was part of that liberty protected by the Fourteenth Amendment against state interference. This ruling had implications for increased protection of the Negro from discriminatory state legislation.

[111] Myrdal, *op. cit.,* II, 450.

stitutional prohibitions against the denial of due process and equal protection of the law.

The case of *Moore v. Dempsey,*[112] which was decided during this period, grew out of a situation which involved the use of illegal practices in court procedure; and it presented the question of mob-dominated trials to the Supreme Court for the first time. The case arose out of the conviction of five Negroes in an Arkansas Court for the murder of a white man. Counsel for the convicted Negroes charged that the trial was conducted under the pressure and influence of a mob and without regard for the constitutional rights of his clients. Only three-quarters of an hour was required for the trial and but five minutes were required for the jury to reach a verdict of guilty. The National Association for the Advancement of Colored People aided in financing the case and became interested in taking it to the United States Supreme Court.[113] An appeal to the United States District Court in Arkansas for a writ of habeas corpus was denied, and appeal from this action was made to and granted by the Supreme Court.

In the majority opinion, written by Mr. Justice Holmes, it was pointed out that where the state provided adequate corrective processes for denials of constitutional rights, the writ of habeas corpus ought not to be allowed. But on the other hand:

> . . . if the case is that the whole proceeding is a mask, that counsel, jury and judge were swept to the fatal end by an irresistible wave of public passion and the State courts failed to correct the wrong, the Supreme Court must secure for the wronged their constitutional rights.[114]

Justice Holmes reprimanded the District Judge for having failed to examine the alleged facts surrounding the trial for himself. This was a dereliction of duty, " for if they be proven true the trial was void." [115] Finding the corrective processes provided by the state grossly inadequate for the protection of the constitutional rights of the convicted persons, an order was issued

---

[112] 261 U. S. 86 (1923).

[113] See *Crisis,* XXI (1920), 65; also XXIII (1921), 72–76.

[114] 261 U. S. 92.

[115] *Ibid.*

reversing the dismissal of the appeal for a writ of habeas corpus. The District Court was ordered to hear the case.[116] This decision is particularly significant for its definition of what constituted a mob-dominated trial. It represents the first effort of the Court to define a trial of this character. Under this definition, convictions, which resulted from "an irresistible wave of public passion," could not be allowed to stand without contravening the guarantees of the Fourteenth Amendment.

With the opinion of the majority, two Justices, McReynolds and Sutherland, could not agree. Justice McReynolds wrote an opinion, concurred in by Justice Sutherland, dissenting from the opinion of the Court. Their opposition was based primarily upon the bad effects which the decision would have upon the enforcement of criminal law in the states. The decision would impose difficulties upon the states in their efforts to enforce the criminal law and to mete out prompt punishment for crime. The District Judge was certainly familiar with local conditions, they felt, and on that basis should have been upheld. Sympathy, aroused by the fact that the petitioners "are poor, ignorant, and black, shouldn't relieve the Court from enforcing essential legal principles." [117]

Between 1920 and 1930 there was a dearth of cases before American courts which involved the Fourteenth Amendment and the Negro. Cases of this type totaled eighteen. Of this number, final decisions were rendered in state courts of last resort in eight cases and in the United States Supreme Court in five cases; the remainder were confined to the lower courts, state and Federal. In eleven of the cases the decision was adverse to the

---

[116] The National Association for the Advancement of Colored People considered the decision "a great achievement in constitutional law." See letter of Attorney Lewis Marshall to the Association in N.A.A.C.P., *Thirteenth Annual Report,* 1922, 27.

[117] 261 U. S. 102. For comment see Little Rock *Arkansas Gazette,* February 21, 1923, 3. Justice McReynolds had a southern background, having been born in Kentucky and appointed to the Court from Tennessee. On the other hand, Justice Sutherland, who concurred with McReynolds, was born in England and was appointed to the Court from the West. See Cortez A. M. Ewing, *Judges of the Supreme Court, 1789–1937* (Minneapolis, 1938), 50–51.

Negro interest involved. Four of the five cases decided by the Supreme Court were favorable to the Negro; and two of the four favorable decisions were *per curiam* decisions applying the rule against segregation ordinances which had been established in the case of *Buchanan v. Warley.* A new departure or application of the Fourteenth Amendment by the Supreme Court is suggested in only one instance—that of mob-dominated trials.

Two factors explain in large measure the infrequency with which the Fourteenth Amendment was invoked by Negroes during this period: the expenses involved in legal action and the burden of proof placed upon those invoking the guarantees of the Fourteenth Amendment to prove the existence of an illegal discrimination. It has been estimated that the cost of taking appeals to the Supreme Court exceeds $3,500.[118] This fact alone tended to discourage, if not prevent, many allegations of disregarded civil rights under the Fourteenth Amendment from being carried before the Court. The burden of proof placed upon appellants to prove allegations of unconstitutional discrimination had a similar effect. In many instances of such discrimination, there was small possibility of developing such proof as would compel judicial interference.[119] Frequently, procedural technicalities made the burden of proof even more difficult.

The Supreme Court revealed a reluctance and a high degree of caution in accepting jurisdiction of cases involving various aspects of the "Negro question" during the decade 1920–1930. Petitions for the writ of certiorari were generally denied.[120] In most instances conclusive effect was given to the findings of state courts of no discrimination by the refusal of the Court to go behind the facts or to consider alleged discriminatory legislation in the light of the intent of the framers. Such a procedure suggested a policy of keeping "hands off" the southern problem wherever possible and of non-interference with the procedure of

---

[118] Fred Minnis, "The Attitude of Federal Courts Toward the Exclusion of Negroes from Jury Service," unpublished master's thesis, Howard University, 1934, 67.

[119] Charles S. Mangum, *The Legal Status of the Negro,* 90.

[120] Gregory and Charlotte Haskins, *The United States Supreme Court, 1927–1928* (Washington, D. C., 1929), 251–54.

state courts. Perhaps fear of the reactions of southern states was a conditioning factor. With the possible exception of the decision in *Moore v. Dempsey*[121] both the application and interpretation of the Fourteenth Amendment by the Supreme Court tended to be conservative. No new or progressive rules of law were formulated; instead, the Court was content to apply, in a restricted manner, conservative interpretations of earlier Justices.

Toward the end of the decade, the Supreme Court was criticized widely for its position in regard to its construction of the Fourteenth Amendment. Conviction of the Court's conservatism, together with the belief that "the color line is the most significant manifestation of the twentieth century and is deepening with the decade,"[122] caused considerable alarm among Negroes. It was felt that the Court tacitly permitted violations of the amendment. There was a wide gulf between theoretical equality before the law and its practice,[123] for real equality could be "neither possible nor desired under the doctrine of separate but equal accommodations."[124] The decisions of the Supreme Court had so emasculated the Fourteenth Amendment that it meant actually nothing, observed one writer; at best it had become a mere "paper guarantee" for the Negro's rights of citizenship.[125] Some were convinced that illegal and extra-legal practices directed against Negroes could not have persisted but for the attitude of the Supreme Court and its conservative interpretation of the Fourteenth Amendment.[126]

---

121 *Supra,* 43–44.

122 Kelly Miller, "Is the Color Line Crumbling?", *Opportunity,* VII (1929), 292.

123 Thelma Bates, "The Status of the Negro in Florida," *Florida Historical Society Quarterly,* VI (1928), 180.

124 William Pickens, "Racial Segregation," *Opportunity,* V (1927), 364 f. In 1925 the National Association for the Advancement of Colored People established a "segregation fund" of $50,000, secured partially from Julius Rosenwald and the Garland Fund to help fight segregation practices in the courts. New York *Times,* December 29, 1925, 16.

125 See address of James W. Johnson in *Crisis,* XXXIV (1927), 224; also Charles H. Wesley, "The Historical Basis of Negro Citizenship," *Opportunity,* II (1924), 359.

126 The decade of the twenties revealed a suspicion of liberal attitudes and

The personnel of the Supreme Court was almost entirely remodeled during the decade 1920–1930. Five of the Justices, some ultra conservative, on the Court in 1929 had been appointed since 1920.[127] Despite these changes in personnel, the Court was generally considered by liberals as reactionary. Both Justices McReynolds and Sutherland were branded as "conservatives" and "stand-patters."[128] On the other hand, those of the liberal tendency, Justices Holmes, Stone, and Brandeis, were called friends of the workingman and the Negro. Justice Holmes had won the high respect of the working class for his progressive attitude as revealed in his dissent in the case of *Lochner v. New York*[129] and of Negroes for his enlightened opinions in *Moore v. Dempsey* and *Nixon v. Herndon.*[130] Early utterances had caused Justice Stone to be branded a liberal, and his appointment to the Court in January, 1925, had resulted in much speculation as to the effect of his presence on the bench upon the decisions of the Court.[131] Of Justice Brandeis, President Wilson said: "He is a friend of all men and a lover of the right; and he knows more than how to talk about the right—he knows how to set it forward in the face of its enemies."[132] These three Justices, Holmes, Stone, and Brandeis, were the "insurgents who stand together against the young conservatives of the Supreme Court"[133] in defense of the rights of man; however, they con-

---

of changes in the status quo. Evidences of persecution of Catholics, Jews, and Negroes were numerous as was also the general disregard of constitutional rights. Jeanette P. Nichols, *Twentieth Century United States* (New York, 1943), 246.

[127] Chief Justice Taft and Justices Sutherland, Butler, Sanford, and Stone.

[128] New York *Times,* September 12, 1922, VII, 3.

[129] 198 U. S. 45 (1905).

[130] *Supra,* 38–39, 43–44. For a discussion of Mr. Justice Holmes' views, see W. H. Hamilton, "The Legal Philosophy of Justice Holmes and Brandeis," *Current History,* XXXIII (1931), 654–60; Joseph P. Pollard, "Justice Holmes Dissents," *Scribner's Magazine,* LXXXV (1929), 22–29.

[131] New York *Times,* January 6, 1925, 1–2.

[132] *Ibid.,* December 8, 1929, V, 12, 23. See Joseph P. Pollard, "Justice Brandeis and the Constitution," *Scribner's Magazine,* LXXXVIII (1930), 11–19.

[133] New York *Times,* December 8, 1929, 12.

stituted a minority on the Court and were unable to make their attitudes prevail.

For more than fifty years prior to 1930, there had been revealed periodically a sentiment which either attacked the validity of the Fourteenth Amendment or urged its modification or repeal. Such an assault was made on the validity of the amendment in 1908. Validity was denied because of the methods employed in securing passage of the resolution of amendment in Congress and in securing ratification by the states. It was contended that in computing two-thirds of each House, representation from states temporarily absent due to the rebellion should have been counted. Moreover, since these states were counted for purposes of ratification, it was only logical that they should have been counted in estimating the two-thirds majority in Congress.[134] Failure to do so rendered the Fourteenth Amendment invalid.

In 1924 the first and only legal attack on the validity of the Fourteenth Amendment was made in the case of *Bolte v. Cohen*[135] which was decided in a United States District Court in Eastern Louisiana. Henry Bolte sought to prevent Walter Cohen, a Negro, from exercising the duties of Comptroller of the Customs for the Port of New Orleans to which he had been appointed. He charged that Cohen was not a citizen of the United States since he was a Negro, for the Fourteenth Amendment, the basis upon which Negroes claimed citizenship, was invalid due to the unconstitutional manner in which it was proposed and ratified. According to Bolte, the amendment had never been proposed by two-thirds of both Houses of Congress, nor ratified by three-fourths of the states.

Judge Foster, the presiding judge, dismissed the bill of complaint and handed down written reasons for doing so. His reasoning quickly disposed of Bolte's argument. Until now, he observed, the whole people had accepted the Fourteenth Amend-

[134] John H. Adriaans, *Has the Negro the Right to Vote?* (Washington, D. C., 1908), 5–9; John W. Burgess, *Reconstruction and the Constitution,* 202–06.

[135] Case No. 17730, U. S. Dist. Ct. E.D. La., 1924. This memorandum decision was never reported; however, a certified typewritten copy of the decision was available.

ment. Moreover, the United States Supreme Court had already pointed out certain rights and guarantees which it offered; and "when the Supreme Court first decided that certain rights were guaranteed and protected by the 14th Amendment, it necessarily then and there affirmed the validity of the amendment." [136]

Something of a short-lived movement for the enforcement of the exact terms of the Fourteenth Amendment was apparent between 1900 and 1910. There were few persons who felt that the amendment was fully enforced in any section of the country. Shortly after 1900 there was some agitation for the enforcement of Section 2 of the amendment by reducing the representation of southern states in Congress.[137] The Republican platform of 1904 contained a plank calling for the introduction of a bill to effect such enforcement; [138] however, after the election, there is no evidence that any effort was put forth to implement this particular plank of the platform.

Increased consciousness of citizenship and its privileges, in part a product of the migration to urban areas, tended to make Negroes more aware of the full extent of the violation of their constitutional rights. Despite the suggestion by some that the Fourteenth Amendment "was outmoded, archaic and had been nullified in the South since 1869," [139] Negroes demanded that the exact provisions of the amendment be enforced.

There were two branches of the Federal Government through which enforcement of the Fourteenth Amendment might be obtained—the legislature and the courts. Legal action between 1920 and 1930 represented an attempt to secure enforcement through the latter, the judicial branch of the government. Here the emphasis was upon the enforcement of the first section of the amendment. The results were generally discouraging; for

---

[136] *Ibid.* See also 18 *Lawyer and Banker* 25; Charles H. Wesley, *loc. cit.*, 322.

[137] Porter, *op. cit.*, 195 ff.; Horace E. Flack, *The Adoption of the Fourteenth Amendment,* 98–116.

[138] Edwin Maxey, "Enforcement of the Fourteenth Amendment," 66 *Albany Law Journal,* 274, 276.

[139] John H. Jones, *The Negroes Are an Economic Problem* (Jamaica, N. Y., 1933), 53, 151–52; Charles W. Collins, *The Fourteenth Amendment and the States,* 166–67, for suggested modifications of the amendment.

even victories before the Supreme Court seemed to result in theoretical rather than practical gains in this respect. And state policies, which virtually nullified the guarantees of the "equal protection" and "due process" clauses, were still countenanced by the Court.

Along with court action, efforts were made throughout the twenties to secure enforcement of the Fourteenth Amendment through the national legislature. These efforts emphasized the enforcement of the second section of the amendment. This section had been inserted into the amendment as a "clumsy substitute" for an outright grant of Negro suffrage. It provided for a reduction in the congressional representation of any state which denied or abridged the right of any male inhabitant to vote in any national election. This clause, except for a brief period around 1904, was apparently forgotten; no efforts had been seriously made to enforce it. Inaction on the part of Congress threatened to nullify it.

Negroes began to press outstanding politicians and Congress for action. Questionnaires were sent to presidential aspirants by the National Association for the Advancement of Colored People in February, 1920, asking their views regarding the enforcement of the Fourteenth Amendment through coercive congressional action.[140] It was pointed out by some that the representation of southern states would be reduced by forty-two representatives if the penalties clause of the amendment was enforced.[141] Non-enforcement and the disfranchisement of Negroes by southern states gave 10,000 votes in Mississippi as much power in the National Government as 97,000 votes in Indiana.[142] The argument was advanced that should states which disfranchised Negroes be confronted with the certainty of reduced representation, restrictions against Negroes would be removed.

In Congress George H. Tinkham, the somewhat eccentric Representative from Massachusetts, proposed a resolution for the enforcement of the second section of the Fourteenth Amendment

---

140 N.A.A.C.P., *Eleventh Annual Report,* 1920, 24. Only two of seventeen persons contacted bothered to reply.

141 Editorial, "Southern Representation," *Crisis,* XIX (1920), 259.

142 Editorial, *Crisis,* XXI (1921), 150.

on December 6, 1920. He asked that the Committee on the Census "be authorized to inquire respecting the extent to which citizens of the United States are denied the right to vote." [143] The question of disfranchisement, he felt, was "one of the most vital questions that can come before this House in this Congress or in any other Congress." [144] To the press he gave the following statement:

> My resolution proposes that an investigation be made of existing disfranchisement in the several States and that where disfranchisement is found as a fact, the representation of those States in the House of Representatives be reduced in accordance with the directions in the Constitution. The issue is purely one of law and order, constitutional enforcement and political equality.[145]

Representative Tinkham felt that a reapportionment of representation should be made which would give southern states representation in proportion to the actual voting population rather than in proportion to the entire population. Unless the new apportionment law which was before Congress took into consideration "the evident disfranchisement as practiced in some states," he was prepared to question the constitutionality of the new House constituted on that law.[146]

Late in December, the Committee of the Census of the House of Representatives held a hearing on the new Reapportionment Bill. Inquiry was made as to disfranchisement in southern states. Representatives of those states denied charges of abridging the political rights of Negro citizens. While it was true that few Negroes voted in the South, it was the result of their "apathetic political nature" rather than of discriminatory practices on the part of the states.[147] However, a Senator from a southern state publicly remarked several years later:

---

143 *Congressional Record,* 66th Cong., 3rd Sess., 1920, LX¹, 11. See also New York *Times,* December 6, 1920, 1.

144 *Ibid.,* LX², 1434.

145 New York *Times,* December 6, 1920, 1.

146 *Ibid.*

147 N.A.A.C.P., *Eleventh Annual Report,* 1920, 28. For the opposite point of view see Leo Alilunas, "Legal Restrictions on the Negro in Politics," *Journal of Negro History,* XXV (1940), 160, 196.

> We have been very careful to obey the letter of the Federal Constitution, but we have been very diligent and astute in violating the spirit of such amendments as would lead the Negro to believe himself the equal of the white man. . . . And we shall continue to conduct ourselves in that way.[148]

Senator Smith of Virginia declared that the South should receive encouragement rather than criticism for preventing Negro domination and control of southern states.[149]

Evidence presented to the Committee of actual disfranchisement of Negro voters proved insufficient to establish the fact of unconstitutional discrimination "beyond a reasonable doubt"; thus, the new Reapportionment Bill, as reported by the Committee, contained no recommendation for reduced representation for any state.[150] An ex-Senator from Mississippi observed that: "The Northern representatives conduct the investigation to the point where they convict the Southern representatives of lying and then stop." [151]

Speaking to the House of Representatives on January 14, 1921, just before the Committee on the Census reported its Bill, Representative Tinkham said:

> It would be a perilous proceeding in these days of revolt against all law and defiance of constitutional authority . . . if representation in this House and in the election of our President is not squarely placed upon a constitutional and lawful basis.
>
> The words "shall be reduced" makes the amendment mandatory, and no apportionment of representation among the several states can be made unless the House of Representatives in good faith at least has attempted to carry out this constitutional mandate. . . . No attempt to carry out this constitutional mandate has been made and no action has been taken . . . and if in this

[148] Remarks of Senator George of Georgia, quoted in *Opportunity,* VI (1928), 132.

[149] Editorial, *Opportunity,* V (1927), 67.

[150] *Congressional Record, op. cit.,* LX², 1648.

[151] Statement of James K. Vardaman, quoted in N.A.A.C.P., *Eleventh Annual Report,* 1920, 29.

> apportionment bill no attempt is made in good faith to carry out these directions, the House of Representatives becomes responsible . . . for the nullification of the Constitution.
>
> . . . .
>
> The power to reduce representation for disfranchisement is the only repressive force in the Constitution to prevent the institutions of the States from gravitating into oligarchies and aristocracies by limiting the elective franchise to a few of the citizens or to a class.[152]

As Tinkham saw it, the Fourteenth Amendment must be applied and obeyed, no matter what the intent had been originally in adding it to the Constitution. The question was neither racial nor sectional; it was merely a question of enforcing the Constitution. The significance of the question was national in scope and demanded a national approach in its solution.[153] Should conditions remain as they were, "voters in States where disfranchisement was great would have much greater political power than voters in States where no disfranchisement existed," declared Representative Tinkham.[154]

When the Committee on the Census failed to report a bill providing for reduced representation in states where disfranchisement existed, Representative Tinkham offered an amendment to the measure which was reported in an effort to accomplish the same purpose.[155] The amendment evoked lengthy and hostile debate on the floor of the House. Representative Mandell of Wyoming expressed the belief that, even if passed, the amendment would have no effect in the enforcement of the Fourteenth Amendment. The proposed amendment to the apportionment bill was finally ruled out of order by the Speaker as not germane to the subject before the House.[156]

---

152 *Congressional Record, op. cit.*, LX^2, 1434–35.

153 *Ibid.*, 1434.

154 *Ibid.*

155 *Ibid.*, 1682.

156 *Ibid.*, 1686, 1688. According to House rules "no motion or proposition on a subject different from that under consideration shall be admitted under color of amendment." Louis Deschler, *Rules of the House of Representatives* (Washington, D. C., 1941), 364. The bill under consideration

Efforts to secure enforcement of the second section of the Fourteenth Amendment were renewed in 1927. By this time the question had assumed more of a political character; more persons were concerned over the over-representation of those states which obviously disfranchised Negro voters.[157] Some urged that the amendment should either be obeyed or repealed; "for disfranchisement had become a national scandal."[158]

On December 5, 1927, Representative Tinkham introduced a resolution which would authorize the Committee on the Census to make "diligent inquiry" into the question of disfranchisement in the United States.[159] His speech before the House on February 28, 1927, urging the House to take some action, was one lasting one hour and thirty minutes. It was ridiculed by a colleague as "the biennial message delivered by the gentleman from cultured Boston."[160] After a lengthy discussion of the significance of the question in which he called non-enforcement "defiantly lawless," he concluded:

> Let us admit freely that the Negro has been abandoned to his political fate. . . . The Constitution, however, can not be abandoned as the Negro has been abandoned. This scandalous disfranchisement, in violation of the Constitution, has been brought repeatedly to the attention of Congress. . . . Yet no action has been taken, and there has been treated with mockery and scorn the suggestion that the Constitution be enforced. This can no longer continue.[161]

The Seventieth Congress took no action on the matter. Thus, Representative Tinkham's efforts of more than seven years to secure enforcement of the Fourteenth Amendment by Congress

---

concerned reapportionment of representation; however, Tinkham's amendment concerned the reduction of representation for disfranchisement.

157 "Nullification," *Opportunity,* V (1927), 97–98.

158 "The Nullified Amendment," *Crisis,* XXXVI (1929), 30; Herbert J. Seligmann, "The Negroes' Influence as a Voter," *Current History,* XXVIII (1928), 231.

159 *Congressional Record,* 70th Cong., 1st Sess., 1928, LXIX[1], 100.

160 *Ibid.,* LXIX[4], 3732.

161 *Ibid.,* 3731. See New York *Times,* January 8, 1928, 12.

bore no fruit. No other member of Congress appears to have been seriously interested in the question. Tinkham's primary interest in the question of disfranchisement, as revealed in his speeches on the subject, was a concern for equality of representation for the states in the national legislature, or as he put it, so that "fraudulent majorities in Southern States [could not] elect the President and control the Congress."[162] While he believed that Negroes were illegally and unjustly disfranchised in southern states, his first consideration was equality of all states in Congress as provided for in the Constitution.

Before the end of the decade hope for the enforcement of the Fourteenth Amendment through congressional action had all but disappeared.[163] Whatever measure of enforcement was to be achieved had to be won in the courts regardless of the limitations which such an approach seemed to imply. The failure of Congress to enact, or to give serious attention to the enactment of, the necessary legislation to enforce the second section of the Fourteenth Amendment revealed the great divergence of interest between the Congress of 1866 and those of the twenties on the question of Negro suffrage. Enfranchisement by congressional action, under authority of Section 2 of the Fourteenth Amendment, would have made unnecessary the protracted court litigation on the subject which continues to the present moment.

---

162 *Congressional Record,* 70th Cong., 1st Sess., 1928, LXIX4, 3731.

163 Kirk Porter, *A History of Suffrage in the United States,* 150–54, supports the thesis that if Federal power had left the states alone, the Negro would have been permanently enfranchised by the southern states. However, the artificial element introduced by the Fourteenth Amendment disturbed the normal process of enfranchisement and made enfranchisement, as attempted under the Fourteenth Amendment, non-enduring.

CHAPTER III

TOWARD A LIBERAL INTERPRETATION, 1931–1935

Political, social, and economic democracy have been widely accepted in the United States for more than a century and a half as a national symbol. On the other hand, popular behavior, and in many situations official action, has established numerous class and color distinctions which stand in sharp contrast to the national ideal. Efforts by Negroes to force the universal acceptance of the basic precepts of democracy in all sections of the United States indicate the extent to which practical affairs depart from the American ideal of a thoroughgoing democracy with its manifold manifestations.

The depression of the early thirties was a national crisis which affected every aspect of the American social and economic structure; no major social institution or human activity escaped its influences. Repercussions of the depression were reflected in the problem of American minority groups and of minority rights; and there resulted renewed effort by minority groups to invoke the constitutional guarantees of the Fourteenth Amendment. Two contrasting trends were apparent in the early thirties which exerted some influence upon the extent and manner in which the Fourteenth Amendment would be applied in regard to minority groups. On the negative side, the depression seemed to call forth race and class conflict in some areas which threatened a total disregard of the constitutional rights of minority groups and the spread of intolerance of minority groups.[1] Majority opinion seemed to indicate a current running against enlarged rights for any group, whether these were deserved or not.

In welcome contrast to this tendency, there appeared during the first four years of the new decade indications of an improve-

[1] Donald Young, *Minority Peoples in the Depression* (New York, 1937), 17; Maurice L. Risen, *Legal Aspects of the Separation of Races in Public Schools* (Philadelphia, 1935), 4.

ment in race relations and race attitudes in both the North and the South.[2] A traveler in the South optimistically reported in 1932: "I found that white persons in the South were taking a much more tolerant attitude toward the Negro. . . . I believe the Negro is much better off educationally and economically in America today than at any time before."[3] The white press of the South, as well as an increasing minority of southern clergymen, lawyers, and intellectuals, evinced an interest in altering the legal procedure which made possible injustices for the Negro in southern courts.[4] Efforts to improve race relations tended to emphasize the fact that mutual cooperation was necessary for the advancement of both races, and that Negroes were citizens entitled to all of the rights and privileges enjoyed by other citizens.[5]

On the whole, race relations tended to improve though the slowness of that development evoked criticism[6] and caused one writer to remark: "Actually in the minds of the majority of white Americans the Negro has no rights and America has no

---

[2] Charles S. Johnson, *Patterns of Negro Segregation,* 320; see Norfolk *Journal and Guide,* July 24, 1937, 9, for results of a survey on race relations conducted by the American Civil Liberties Union.

[3] Observations of Dr. J. E. Holloway, Director of Census and Statistics of the Union of South Africa, New York *Times,* November 26, 1932, 17.

[4] Henry J. McGuinn, "Equal Protection and Fair Trials in Maryland," *Journal of Negro History,* XXIV (1939), 145. Majority sentiment in the South remained that expressed by Senator E. D. (Cotton Ed) Smith of South Carolina, who felt that "I cannot and will not be a party to the recognition of the Fourteenth and Fifteenth Amendments." *Negro Year-Book,* 1937–1938, 103.

[5] Donald Young, *American Minority Peoples* (New York, 1932), 190; *Negro Year-Book,* 1937–1938, 103; American Civil Liberties Union, *Black Justice* (New York, 1931). For a thorough analysis of the techniques employed in the interracial movement during the thirties, see Paul E. Baker, *Negro-White Adjustment* (Pittsfield, Mass., 1937).

[6] W. O. Brown, "Interracial Cooperation: Some of Its Problems," *Opportunity,* XI (1932), 272, held that the movement tended to be too conservative and failed to come to terms with the fundamental problem of the unequal placement of the Negro in the American social order. A belief in new racial attitudes and in an improvement of conditions for Negroes was based upon faith and hope, not upon practical achievement.

obligation to him."[7] Measured in terms of actual results, the movement for improved race relations of the early thirties was disappointing to most Negroes; however, a necessary function was performed by the effort in raising problems of discriminatory practices and inequality in regard to the Negro before the American people. The creation of a mass opinion favorable to the enforcement of the Fourteenth Amendment was necessary before there could be much hope that favorable court decisions would be handed down. In the final analysis, the Fourteenth Amendment "is worth whatever the courts and legislature choose to make it from time to time. And what they choose to make it is no more and no less than what the consensus of opinion—not of enlightened opinion mind you, but of general opinion, of mass opinion . . . wants to see it made."[8]

During the early years of the thirties there was increased activity on the part of Negroes to secure the full enforcement of the Fourteenth Amendment through court action. Despite the limited success of such an approach during the twenties, two significant factors—a tendency toward an improvement in race relations and organized Negro protest and effort—indicated greater success in the early thirties. Evidence of an organized movement of protest on the part of Negroes against the disparity between Negro and white citizens was more than apparent. The fact that the Negro developed more rapidly than did his opportunities for participation in American society made a movement of protest all but inevitable.

One writer warned that discriminatory treatment:

> . . . is moving thousands of Negroes who had previously been quiescent to active indignation. . . . The situation as a whole, is moving toward greater intensity, and there is no wisdom in closing our eyes to the unwelcome fact.[9]

Another contemporary observed a change in the Negro's intel-

---

[7] Newell L. Sims, "Techniques of Race Adjustment," *Journal of Negro History,* XVI (1931), 84.

[8] H. L. Mencken, "Notes on Negro Strategy," *Crisis,* XLI (1934), 289.

[9] Editorial, "The Rising Tide of Negro Protest," *Christian Century,* XLVII (1930), 1140.

lectual conviction from an attitude of compromise to one of challenge. The twin doctrines of protest and resistance were strongly advocated.[10] There was some concern over the possibility that discontent and protest over their unequal status would lead Negroes to the use of force as the only means of achieving their rights. "Certainly there was enough possibility in this direction," declared one writer, "to cause concern,"[11] for the attitude of the average white person was such that it indicated no change in the Negro's status.[12]

Specifically, Negro protest was aimed at the enforcement of his rights of American citizenship as guaranteed by the Fourteenth Amendment. Tersely stated, the Negro's goal was "to receive of the government and of the law the same treatment accorded the genuine citizen—no more, no less, and no others."[13] Equality before the law as guaranteed by the Constitution was in danger of being lost by default.[14] This was most evident in regard to educational opportunities and equal justice before the courts in southern jurisdictions. Whereas the Negro had protested against segregation or color distinction between 1920 and 1930, he now placed greater emphasis upon equal rights and equality before the law.

The value of a movement of protest in securing equal rights was seriously questioned in some quarters. As one opinion expressed it, "the fight against discrimination of all kinds . . . provides the stuff out of which the Negro liberation movement is created"; however, the most effective approach to the problem was an economic approach which must center around the crea-

---

[10] V. F. Calverton, "The Negro's New Belligerent Attitude," *Current History,* XXX (1929), 1088.

[11] E. A. Schaal, "Will the Negro Rely on Force?", *Crisis,* XL (1933), 9.

[12] While charges of excess radicalism were leveled at Negro protest, it appears that radicalism had a rather indifferent success among Negroes as far as numbers are concerned. Such conversion to radicalism as did occur was largely limited to a few of the younger, urbanized, intellectual leaders. See Donald Young, *Minority Peoples in the Depression,* 160–61.

[13] Kelly Miller, "Government and the Negro," *Annals of the American Academy of Political and Social Science,* CXL (1928), 104.

[14] Norfolk *Journal and Guide,* July 6, 1935, 6.

tion of an integral unity between Negro and white labor.[15] It was also held that the theory of the Negro, "that Negroes under the American system have certain inalienable rights and when deprived of them they can get them back by making an uproar," was unsound.[16] Moreover, in the face of a tendency toward revulsion against liberty everywhere and the feeling that "the Negro has gone far enough, that he already has as much as he deserves and should be content for a while," prospects for Negroes to enlarge or obtain the full exercise of their constitutional rights seemed negligible.[17] One Negro leader was convinced that protest should be accompanied by the practice of overwhelming the Supreme Court with cases involving "the blatant and impudent discrimination" against Negroes to compel decisions which would make discrimination impossible.[18]

The Negro movement of protest of the early thirties revealed an organized effort and cooperation among Negroes[19] which was absent during most of the preceding decade.[20] Effective collective action and a sense of solidarity were, in large measure, the product of the failure to secure the enforcement of the Fourteenth Amendment during the twenties. Perhaps the first successful demonstration of this cohesion was made in the

---

15 James S. Allen, *The Negro Question in the United States* (New York, 1936), 10.

16 Mencken, *loc. cit.*, 289.

17 *Ibid.*

18 W. E. B. DuBois, "Does the Negro Need Separate Schools?", *Journal of Negro Education,* IV (1935), 332.

19 There is little evidence that Negroes and other minority groups cooperated to any appreciable extent in the struggle for an extension of their constitutional rights. Donald Young, *Minority Peoples in the Depression,* 140, attributes this to the fact that minority peoples have too little in common "to permit their standing shoulder to shoulder except in sporadic instances."

20 Guy B. Johnson, "Negro Racial Movements and Leadership in the United States," *American Journal of Sociology,* XLIII (1937), 59, develops the thesis that a real unity and cohesion in Negro life is impossible because of the benevolence, good will, and philanthropy which have characterized the American bi-racial system and which have relieved the Negro from the necessity of relying upon his own efforts. See also Paul Lewinson, *Race, Class, and Party,* 127–31.

protest against the confirmation of Judge John J. Parker of the United States Circuit Court as Justice of the Supreme Court because of his alleged views and remarks which were prejudicial to the constitutional rights of Negroes.[21] While the opposition of Negroes cannot be considered the deciding factor in defeating confirmation, its influence appears to have been a definite contributing factor.

Leadership of organized Negro effort during this period tended to center around the National Association for the Advancement of Colored People. The purposes of this organization were threefold: (1) to educate America to extend full rights and opportunities to Negroes; (2) to conduct an aggressive campaign of court action to fight injustices against Negroes; and (3) to defeat the enactment of discriminatory legislation.[22] The Association represented the point of view that:

> . . . either the Negro will become a full fledged American citizen the equal of every other citizen in legal rights, political power, and opportunity and social recognition . . . or democracy in America will die and democracy in the world receive a mortal blow.[23]

The southern press did not underestimate the leadership which the Association gave to the Negro race. It warned that this leadership was dangerous to the white South, for it was shrewd, bold, and able, and would insist upon the recognition of the Negro in the South.[24]

Much of the energy of the National Association for the Advancement of Colored People was spent in legal action. The Association furnished legal aid in cases where race prejudice had resulted in injustices to Negroes, feeling that favorable decisions would lead to an increase in the civil rights of Negroes

---

[21] Walter White, "The Negro and the Supreme Court," *Harper's Magazine,* CLXII (1931), 238; Robert E. Jack, *History of the National Association for the Advancement of Colored People* (Boston, 1943), 90–91.

[22] Fitzhugh L. Styles, *Negroes and the Law* (Boston, 1937), 173; Charles S. Johnson, *op. cit.,* 192; Editorial, *Opportunity,* V (1927), 223 f.

[23] W. E. B. DuBois, "Opinion," *Crisis,* XXVIII (1924), 103 f.

[24] Charleston (S. C.) *News and Courier,* April 28, 1936, 4.

throughout the United States and establish controlling precedents in the communities affected. In 1932 the National Office and its 327 branches spent about $124,000 in the campaign to secure the rights of American citizenship to Negroes.[25] Between 1931 and 1934 the Association carried two cases involving the Negro and the Fourteenth Amendment before the United States Supreme Court and won favorable decisions in both instances.[26]

There were those who criticized both the leadership furnished by the National Association for the Advancement of Colored People and its defensive, legalistic program. One Negro leader held that the mere negative program to avoid segregation should be supplanted by one of a more positive character which offered the Negro economic guidance.[27] "Today, this organization . . . finds itself in a time of crisis and change," he stated, "without a program, without effective organization, without executive officers . . . to guide the National Association for the Advancement of Colored People in the right direction." [28] A criticism of the Association's program and its too exclusive reliance upon court decisions was offered by a southern white sociologist of the liberal school who declared:

> Now, while this legalistic approach has been successful in the sense . . . that it has won numerous important legal cases—some of them United States Supreme Court decisions involving new precedents—it is doubtful whether it has brought the Negro any nearer his goal. . . . One wonders then, whether its chief value aside from its value in actually obtaining racial rights, has not been to serve as a catharsis for those discontented, impatient souls who, while they see no hope for normal

[25] N.A.A.C.P., *Twenty-Third Annual Report,* 1932, 53.

[26] *Nixon v. Condon,* 286 U. S. 73; *Hollins v. Oklahoma,* 295 U. S. 394.

[27] Opinion of W. E. B. DuBois, editor of the *Crisis;* see *Crisis,* XXXIX (1932), 218. For an extensive analysis of the program of the National Association for the Advancement of Colored People see Gunnar Myrdal, *An American Dilemma,* II, 819–36.

[28] Letter of resignation of W. E. B. DuBois to the Board of Directors of the National Association for the Advancement of Colored People, June 28, 1934, quoted in *Crisis,* XLI (1934), 245.

> participation in American life, feel that they must never give in and admit that they are beaten down spiritually.[29]

Moreover, the leadership furnished the Negro appeared to lack the whole-hearted support of southern Negroes because it lacked a realistic approach in its efforts to win the exercise of constitutional rights by Negroes.[30]

No matter how numerous the criticisms made of the National Association for the Advancement of Colored People or how valid they might have been, these criticisms cannot obscure a significant development which was taking place in Negro life during the early thirties. One cannot read the literature of the period without being led to the conclusion that Negroes throughout the United States had become really vocal for the first time. The failure to enforce the provisions of the Fourteenth Amendment during the twenties and the consequent discrimination, segregation, and deprivation of rights of citizenship which lack of enforcement entailed, undoubtedly served to foster the idea that protest and organized effort were the most effective means of compelling a better enforcement of the amendment. When compared with the effort to enforce the Fourteenth Amendment of the decade 1920–1930, the movement of protest of the early thirties reveals two sharp contrasts: it was more racially organized and controlled and it was more of a purely Negro movement than the earlier effort. Furthermore, there was a tendency to appeal to Negroes for financial support rather than to appeal almost exclusively to philanthropy.[31] Despite these differences, both movements are to be considered as significant parts of the larger effort—the effort to secure a practical application of the Fourteenth Amendment. Any study of the actual interpretation and application of the Fourteenth Amendment, as revealed in

---

[29] Guy B. Johnson, *loc. cit.*, 66–67.

[30] Letter of Guy B. Johnson to the *Crisis,* XLVI (1939), 271.

[31] Even during this period a portion of the funds used by the National Association for the Advancement of Colored People to finance its program came from philanthropic sources. For example, beginning in 1930, the American Fund for Public Service began contributions to the Association to help finance its program for the protection of the Negro's constitutional rights. See Paul E. Baker, *Negro-White Adjustment,* 82.

cases involving the Negro between 1931 and 1935, must take into consideration the influence of Negro organization and protest.

Efforts to secure the enforcement of the Fourteenth Amendment between 1931 and 1935 tended to center around two major subject areas: fair trials for Negroes, with their many manifestations, and the participation of Negroes in primary elections in southern states. In both instances the equal protection clause of the Fourteenth Amendment served as the constitutional basis for legal action. Twelve of the nineteen cases involving the Negro and the Fourteenth Amendment which were decided during this period involved the application and interpretation of this clause of the amendment.[32] Equal protection of equal laws for all American citizens became the ideal and the goal of Negroes in their effort to enforce the provisions of the Fourteenth Amendment.

Fair Trials for Negroes

The question of what constitutes a fair trial has never been categorically answered by the courts. However, there are some basic conditions which should prevail, the absence of which immediately marks a trial as unfair. Among these conditions are: trials uninfluenced by the pressure of the mob spirit; jurors who are free of prejudice in regard to the accused; adequate counsel for the accused; and the lack of discrimination against members of the same race as the accused in regard to jury service. Frequently, in criminal trials in the South involving Negroes, these basic elements of a fair trial have not obtained. The necessity of invoking the Fourteenth Amendment to assure Negroes of fair trials in southern courts is easily recognized when one recalls that criminal law and its application is largely a matter of state administration.

In 1931, eight years after Mr. Justice Holmes' opinion in the case of *Moore v. Dempsey,*[33] the question of a mob-dominated trial was again before the Federal courts in the case of *Downer*

---

[32] Between 1920 and 1930 the "due process" clause was the clause most frequently invoked by Negroes.

[33] *Supra,* 43–44.

v. Dunaway.[34] The case arose in Elberton, Georgia, where Downer, a Negro, was arrested and indicted for rape. It was necessary for the Governor of Georgia to call out state troops to forestall mob action. During the trial before a state court, which resulted in conviction and the death sentence, a mob gathered before the courthouse and threatened lynching if the prisoner were acquitted. The Commission on Interracial Agencies, feeling that an impartial justice had not been rendered, became instrumental in securing an appeal from the state court to the Federal court.[35] Appeal to the United States District Court for a writ of habeas corpus was denied on the ground that the state of Georgia provided ample corrective processes for any disregard of Downer's rights.[36] Appeal was made from this action to the United States Circuit Court of Appeals for the Fifth Circuit.

The Circuit Court declared the conviction void because the defendant had been deprived of a fundamental constitutional right—due process of law as guaranteed by the Fourteenth Amendment. It was of little importance that the state of Georgia provided ample corrective processes; in the case under review, the trial court had not made them available to the defendant. Furthermore, "it was the duty of the trial judge to refuse to put the accused to trial in the presence of a mob whose violence was prevented only by the presence of troops."[37] A trial conducted under these conditions "cannot be other than void" for impartial justice was impossible. In the opinion of the court the writ applied for should have been issued; thus, the order of the District Court dismissing the suit was reversed.[38]

Fair trial must mean that trial jurors are free of any racial prejudices that might preclude their rendering a fair and im-

---

[34] 53 Fed. (2d) 586 (C.C.A. 5th Ct., Ga.).

[35] Baker, *op. cit.*, 58–63.

[36] 53 Fed. (2d) 587.

[37] *Ibid.*, 589.

[38] The rule applied here was essentially that established in *Moore v. Dempsey,* 261 U. S. 96 (1923). Here, however, the opinion seems to emphasize, not mob domination, but the "substantial" denial to the defendant of the corrective processes of the state though such processes were available.

partial verdict. And the court's refusal to permit the questioning of prospective jurors as to the holding of such prejudices is a denial of due process of law. This position was taken by the United States Supreme Court in 1931 in a case involving a Negro defendant on trial for the murder of a white man in the District of Columbia.[39] Counsel for the Government contended that allowing questions to jurors as to racial or religious prejudices would be detrimental to the administration of law in United States Courts.

Mr. Justice Holmes, who wrote the majority opinion, felt that the argument of counsel for the Government was untenable. He stated: "No surer way could be devised to bring the processes of justice into disrepute than to permit it to be thought that persons entertaining disqualifying prejudices were allowed to serve as jurors."[40] No matter what privileges were accorded Negroes in a community, reasoned Justice Holmes, the mere taking for granted of the non-existence of such prejudices "was a grave risk in a life and death issue." The judgment of the lower court, disallowing the questioning of prospective jurors as to the holding of racial prejudices, was reversed because it denied to the defendant due process of law.

In a dissenting opinion Mr. Justice McReynolds took essentially the same position he had taken eight years earlier in his dissent in *Moore v. Dempsey*.[41] He expressed the belief that the decision of the Court would contribute to the difficulties of enforcing criminal law, "already scandalously ineffective," by "magnifying theoretical possibilities."[42] Moreover, the knowledge of the local courts as to local racial conditions was so far superior to that of the Supreme Court that it should have been relied upon.

It is an elementary principle of American constitutional law that a man accused of crime, no matter what his race, color, or creed, must be given the fairest trial possible. Frequently, a person accused of crime is too poor to employ counsel to advise and represent him. To prevent jeopardy to the constitutional

---

[39] *Aldridge v. United States*, 283 U. S. 308.

[40] *Ibid.*, 315.

[41] *Supra*, 44.

[42] 283 U. S. 318.

rights of persons so situated, courts are authorized to provide counsel. The mandate of the Fourteenth Amendment requires that a person accused of crime must be furnished counsel; otherwise, a denial of due process of law results. Sometimes the problem has arisen as to what constitutes a denial of right of counsel. The problem resolves itself into the following: whether or not the court is definite in its assignment of counsel and whether or not counsel is allowed sufficient time to consult with the accused before going to trial. While persons accused of crime and furnished counsel by the court have no doubt suffered from the appointment of youthful, inexperienced counsel, youth and inexperience are not, in themselves, sufficient to sustain allegations of denial of right of counsel.[43]

Problems connected with the assignment of counsel by the court have given rise to a great deal of litigation in regard to criminal cases involving poor, ignorant Negroes in the South. The dearth of Negro lawyers in the South, together with race friction, has led almost invariably to the assignment of white attorneys in such cases. Negroes convicted under such circumstances have sometimes alleged a denial of "adequate representation" by counsel and thus a denial of a constitutional right guaranteed by the Fourteenth Amendment.[44] This question was raised in *Downer v. Dunaway,* discussed above, where counsel appointed by the court failed to ask for a change of venue in the face of mob influence upon the trial of his Negro client. The United States Circuit Court of Appeals held that an accused person who is unable to employ counsel "is entitled to be de-

---

[43] Charles S. Mangum, *The Legal Status of the Negro,* 340–41.

[44] An interesting case involving this issue arose in Indiana in 1941 where a white youth, accused of being an accomplice to burglary and murder and being unable to employ counsel, had a young Negro attorney appointed by the court to defend him. Upon his conviction, the youth appealed to the Federal courts claiming a denial of right of counsel and due process under the Fourteenth Amendment in that the counsel appointed to represent him was a Negro and inexperienced. Rightly enough, the court ruled: "It is legal competency, not social status, distinction, or qualification that counts and controls." Moreover, the fact that the counsel was colored should neither have prejudiced the defendant nor prevented his having a fair trial. *Achtien v. Dowd,* 117 Fed. (2d) 989 (C.C.A. 7th Ct., Ind.).

fended in all his rights as fully and to the same extent as is [one] who is able to employ his own counsel."[45] Counsel's failure to defend the accused's rights, whether through ignorance or through a too narrow construction placed upon his appointment by the court, could neither be attributed to the accused, nor considered a waiver of a constitutional right. The court found that the petitioner had not been "adequately represented by counsel."

The first opportunity for a ruling by the United States Supreme Court on the issue of what legally constituted a denial of counsel and to what extent such a denial is prohibited by the Fourteenth Amendment was presented in the case of *Powell v Alabama,*[46] the first of the two *Scottsboro* cases. The case tended to focus national attention upon every aspect of the southern judicial system and the treatment accorded Negro defendants in southern jurisdictions. This case is a good example of the extent to which mass protest can be mobilized against alleged disregard of the basic rights of equal justice as set forth in the first section of the Fourteenth Amendment.[47]

The case arose out of the indictment of Powell and eight other Negro youths for the rape of two white girls of questionable character in Alabama. Conducted in the midst of strongly hostile public feeling, the trials lasted three days and resulted in conviction and the imposition of the death penalty. Motion for a new trial was overruled by the trial court and the judgment was confirmed by the Supreme Court of Alabama. A writ of certiorari was granted by the United States Supreme Court to review the judgment of the Supreme Court of Alabama.

Counsel for Powell held that the trial before the courts of Alabama had resulted in the denial of the constitutional rights of his client on three counts: (1) a fair and impartial trial was not afforded; (2) there had been a denial of the right of counsel and of the opportunity to prepare for trial; and (3) there had

---

[45] 53 Fed. (2d) 586.

[46] 278 U. S. 46 (1932).

[47] Washington *Afro-American,* April 22, 1933, 1–2; Birmingham *News,* November, 7, 1932, 2; Baker, *op. cit.,* 67–72; New York *Times,* November 8, 1932, 11.

been a systematic exclusion of Negroes from both the grand jury and trial jury which had indicted and convicted Powell. These denials, counsel for the petitioner argued, constituted a denial of due process of law.[48] Counsel for Alabama urged upon the Court the argument that due process of law should be interpreted in such a manner as not to restrict the states in their methods of administering justice. Moreover, the law of the jurisdiction where the offense was committed and where the trial was held should be the deciding factor in determining what constituted due process of law.[49]

The majority opinion, handed down on November 7, 1932, was written by Mr. Justice Sutherland.[50] Though three constitutional issues were presented to the Court in this case—lack of a fair and impartial trial, denial of right of counsel, and the systematic exclusion of Negroes from Jury service—the Court elected to decide the case on the issue of denial of right of counsel. This represented a departure on the part of the Court from its practice of refusing to determine a new constitutional issue wherever a case may be determined on an issue already decided by a previous ruling. Precedents had already been established on the questions of the exclusion of Negroes from jury service and on mob-dominated trials;[51] nevertheless, the Court elected to decide the case before it on the new constitutional issue—the denial of the right of counsel.[52]

In the majority opinion written by Mr. Justice Sutherland, it was emphasized that the Court would consider only the question

---

[48] 287 U. S. 46.

[49] *Ibid.,* 47. This contention appears to be based upon the ruling set up by the Supreme Court in *Hurtado v. California,* 110 U. S. 516, 535.

[50] Justice Sutherland had dissented from the majority opinion in *Moore v. Dempsey* in 1923 in which the issue of mob-dominated trials, one of the issues involved in the present case, was before the Court. *Supra,* 44.

[51] *Supra,* 9–10, 43–44.

[52] Alfred J. Cidella and Irwin J. Kaplan, "Discrimination Against Negroes in Jury Service," 29 *Illinois Law Review,* 506, 507, contend that this departure from practice reveals the Supreme Court's "evasiveness and tendency to turn cases on a harmless issue," for reversal of the Supreme Court of Alabama on the selected issue would cause less southern resentment than reversal on either of the other two issues presented.

of the denial of right of counsel. Two questions had to be answered in considering the issue: whether there had been a denial of counsel and whether such denial contravened the "due process" clause of the Fourteenth Amendment. First, the state's contention that counsel had been provided by the trial court was examined. The sole evidence offered by the state of Alabama in support of the contention was the trial court judge's appointment of "all of the members of the bar" to defend the accused Negro youths. Such a designation of counsel, Justice Sutherland declared, "was little more than an expansive gesture imposing no substantial or definite obligation upon anyone." Moreover, it was "so indefinite and so close upon the trial," he continued, "as to amount to a denial of effective and substantial aid in that regard."[53] An examination of the circumstances and proceedings of the trial could lead to but one conclusion:

> . . . that during the most critical part of the proceedings . . . when consultation, investigation, and preparation were vitally important, the defendants did not have the aid of counsel in any real sense [though they were] entitled to counsel during this period as during the actual trial. We hold the defendants were not accorded the right of counsel in any substantial sense.[54]

According to the view taken by Justice Sutherland in this case, right of counsel was interpreted to mean that persons charged with serious crime should not only have counsel designated, but that sufficient time should be allowed for consultation with counsel and the preparation of defense. In the first part of the decision, the Court defined the term right of counsel for the first time. Its essential elements were designation of counsel to represent the accused before the court and the allotment of sufficient time after appointment to investigate, consult with the accused, and prepare the defense. The absence of the latter element constituted a denial of the right of counsel as effectively as if no appointment had been made.

Having determined that the right of counsel had been denied

[53] 287 U. S. 57.

[54] *Ibid.*, 57–58.

Powell and the other eight Negro defendants by the courts of Alabama, Justice Sutherland proceeded to inquire whether such a denial contravened due process under the Fourteenth Amendment. Despite the fact that the question had never been determined by the Supreme Court, he felt the right in question was as fundamental in character as the right to compensation for property taken for public use which the Court had determined was protected by the "due process" clause of the amendment. "It is the duty of the court, whether requested or not, to assign counsel" in a capital case where the defendant is unable to employ counsel. The fulfillment of this requirement was "a necessary requisite of due process of law [and] one of the immutable principles of justice," concluded the opinion, "which the states may not disregard."[55] Therefore, the decision of the Supreme Court of Alabama was reversed because it countenanced a contravention of due process of law as prohibited by the Fourteenth Amendment.

Justices Butler and McReynolds refused to follow the reasoning of the majority. In a separate opinion written by Butler and concurred in by McReynolds, it was held that there had been no denial of right of counsel in that counsel originally appointed by the court had had sufficient time for preparing the defense. But more important, these two dissenting reactionaries deplored the fact that the Court had ruled that the right denied was within the meaning of the Fourteenth Amendment. The ruling that the right of counsel had been denied would have been sufficient, they thought. But by broadening the interpretation of the amendment to include this as one of the protected rights, the beginning was made for "an extension of federal authority into a field hitherto occupied exclusively by the several states."[56] The result of such an extension of authority would inevitably mean the subjection of criminal procedure in state courts to review by the Federal judiciary.

The decision of the Supreme Court demanding a new trial for

---

[55] *Ibid.*, 58.

[56] *Ibid.*, 76. For Justice Butler see Richard J. Purcell, "Mr. Justice Pierce Butler," *Catholic Educational Review*, XLII (1944), 193–215, 327–41, 420–32.

the Scottsboro boys was accepted by Negroes and liberals as "the best type of American justice" and as "a landmark in the path of Negro progress."[57] Federal intervention such as that exercised by the Supreme Court in this case was necessary to guarantee full justice to Negro defendants in assault cases before southern courts.[58] The basis for the Court's decision was quite clear and simple, thought one editor, who declared: "The idea upon which the decision is based is that the Negro defendants did not have their day in court in the true sense of that phrase."[59] Arthur G. Hayes, a distinguished lawyer of the American Civil Liberties Union, was convinced that the Supreme Court's reversal of the Supreme Court of Alabama was forced by mass pressure and mass protest.[60]

The real significance of the decision in the first *Scottsboro* case, as it concerns the Negro and the Fourteenth Amendment, was perhaps the fact that it represented an application of the limitations of the Fourteenth Amendment to a state criminal trial. The decision represents but the second such application of the Fourteenth Amendment by the United States Supreme Court between 1920 and 1932. The first such application in this period was that in *Moore v. Dempsey* in 1923.[61] Throughout this period of twelve years, the Court had been "insistently cautious in subjecting State criminal trials to the limitations of the Fourteenth Amendment."[62] In view of this fact, the decision represented a broadening of the application of the amendment by the Supreme Court and contained implications for a "better justice" for Negroes accused of crime before southern courts.

---

[57] New York *Times,* November 8, 1932, 11; Editorial, "Scottsboro," *Opportunity,* XI (1933), 134.

[58] New York *Herald Tribune,* November 8, 1932, 20.

[59] New York *Sun,* November 8, 1932, 14.

[60] New York *Times,* November 8, 1932, 11.

[61] 261 U. S. 86.

[62] Felix Frankfurter, "A Notable Decision," New York *Times,* November 13, 1932, II, 2. Frankfurter holds that the Supreme Court will still act with caution and hesitation, but it "will not condone judicial-murder in permitting the disregard of due process of law in criminal trials."

Exclusion from Juries

Periodic attacks have been made upon the southern jury system by Negroes and their sympathizers since the late seventies. A study of Supreme Court decisions on the subject prior to 1930 reveals that such attacks were generally unsuccessful in that they failed to destroy the practice of the systematic exclusion of Negroes from jury service. During the period 1931–1935, it became obvious that Negroes had launched a concerted attack against the exclusion of Negroes from jury service in the South. One writer found the question of Negroes on juries "one of the most bitterly fought and most frequently litigated phases of the whole problem of race relations in the South."[63] Its importance was attributed to the fact that the question involved many social, economic, and psychological problems. The jury campaign of the early thirties revealed two characteristics which set it off from earlier efforts: it was a carefully planned campaign and it was largely the product of organized Negro effort. Attacking the exclusion of Negroes from juries in the South, from the Negro's point of view, was but another attempt to secure the enforcement of the Fourteenth Amendment.

The factors which called forth the campaign to win equal protection of the law for Negroes, as it applied to service on juries in southern jurisdictions, were varied indeed. In part this was one aspect of the larger movement of protest by Negroes for a full enjoyment of the rights and privileges of American citizenship. Realizing that Negroes played no part in the administration of justice in the South and that when a Negro faced a white jury, he usually had to "settle the charge against himself as an individual but also the traditional charges against his race,"[64] it became necessary to force the inclusion of Negroes on jury panels.

The evidence seems to indicate that prior to 1935 discrimination against Negroes in regard to jury service was general in southern jurisdictions. One investigator stated: "It seems most probable that this injustice is much more frequent in practice

---

63 Cidella and Kaplan, *loc. cit.*, 499.

64 Editorial, Atlanta *Daily World*, July 13, 1933, quoted in Rollins Chambliss, *What Negro Papers of Georgia Say About Some Social Problems*, University of Georgia, *Bulletin*, XXXV (1933), No. 2, 36–37.

than the number of appealed cases indicates."[65] Law enforcement officers in some southern states admitted that "Negro jurors are rare enough to cause comment in courthouse corridors."[66] However, the rarity of Negro jurors was explained as being the result of Negroes' lack of desire to serve rather than of any discriminatory practice of the state.[67] Opposition to Negro jurors, to a great extent, was engendered by the conviction of the Negro's inability to serve and the fear that the contacts with whites, which jury service necessitated, had the savor of social equality.[68] Here and there enlightened opinion urged that "the states should cease to give grounds for the objection of exclusion of Negroes from juries" and that neither the social standing of white attorneys, who appealed to Negro jurors for a verdict, nor the well-being of white jurors, who sat beside them, would be impaired by having them serve.[69]

Indirect methods were largely employed to effect the exclusion of Negroes from jury service in southern states. This was necessary since the Supreme Court had ruled more than a half century before that state legislation restricting jury service to

[65] United States National Commission on Law Observation and Law Enforcement, *Report on Lawlessness in Law Enforcement* (Washington, D. C., 1931), 285.

[66] Oklahoma City *Daily Oklahoman,* May 14, 1935, 10.

[67] Some judicial officials claimed that when called for jury service, Negroes generally asked to be excused stating "they do not care to serve" and they were generally excused. It appears that such requests to be excused were sometimes inspired by fears of local reaction against Negroes who served on juries. *Negro Year-Book,* 1931–1932, 58. See also Gilbert T. Stephenson, *Race Distinctions in American Law,* 253–71. In some instances state officials admitted that Negroes were never permitted to serve though they were not barred from jury service by statute. Tulsa *Daily News,* May 14, 1935, 9.

[68] A judge in Owensboro, Kentucky, suggested as a solution of the jury question the practice of having Negro juries try Negro defendants. When brought to trial it would be optional with a Negro defendant whether he would be tried by a Negro or white jury. It is probable that such a practice would be declared unconstitutional by the Supreme Court. For an account of this proposal, see *Negro Year-Book,* 1931–1932, 61.

[69] Address of Henry M. Armistead before the Bar Association of Arkansas, June 2, 1933, in Bar Association of Arkansas, *Proceedings,* 1933, 112.

whites was a direct violation of the Fourteenth Amendment.[70] By 1931, state statutes establishing requirements for jurors generally required that jurors be qualified electors. Since it was difficult for Negroes to become electors in southern states, they were effectively disqualified from jury service.[71] A similar result was achieved by granting wide discretionary powers to officials who drew up jury panels. Such methods adopted by southern jurisdictions were successful both in excluding Negroes from jury service and in evading the earlier decisions of the Supreme Court on the matter between 1879 and 1934. So effective were they that the Supreme Court, which had ruled, in 1879, that race could not be made the basis for denying service on juries, found it necessary to order new trials for Negro defendants in only two instances.[72]

Attacks on the southern jury system were made through both the Negro press[73] and the courts. The position taken by the Federal courts on this issue indicated that court action involved serious difficulties and limitations. Since discrimination against Negroes in jury service, in the absence of statutory provisions to that effect, was the product of the discretionary powers of officials, recourse could be had to the Supreme Court only after appeal through the highest state court. State courts rarely found evidence sustaining allegations of discrimination in jury service on the basis of race and color. Moreover, cases which reached the United States Supreme Court after the journey through the state courts had resulted in little relief for the Negro petitioner. It was the practice of the Court either to affirm the decision of the state court or to give conclusive effect to the state court's findings of fact on the question.[74] Whatever remedy court action

---

[70] *Strauder v. West Virginia,* 100 U. S. 303 (1879).

[71] For a brief survey of state statutes establishing requirements for jurors, see Fred Minnis, "The Attitude of Federal Courts on the Exclusion of Negroes from Jury Service," unpublished master's thesis, Howard University, 1934, 29–35.

[72] *Carter v. Texas,* 177 U. S. 442 (1900) and *Rogers v. Alabama,* 192 U. S. 226 (1904).

[73] See following issues of the Norfolk *Journal and Guide,* August 12, 1933, 10; October 12, 1933, 1; December 23, 1933, 1.

[74] Cidella and Kaplan, *loc. cit.,* 502–3. It should be kept in mind that in

offered, as a means of eliminating this disregard of the Fourteenth Amendment through methods of indirection, was to be an expensive one.

Perhaps the first jury case to attract national attention during this period was the case of *Lee v. State*,[75] decided in Maryland in 1932. Euel Lee, a Negro, was indicted for murder, tried, and convicted by all white juries and sentenced to death. He charged a violation of equal protection of law under the Fourteenth Amendment in that Negroes had been unconstitutionally excluded from the juries by which he had been indicted and convicted. In Maryland the method used for selecting jurors was by a judge " from his contacts and information " of persons who were honest, sober, reputable, and taxpayers. The judge who selected jurors for the court in which Lee was tried had never selected a Negro juror over a period of twenty-six years. He contended that he had worked no discrimination against Negroes and that the sole purpose of his selections was " the orderly administration of justice." [76] Commenting on this method of selecting juries, one editor remarked:

> The County Judge who selects the panels seems to have done his duty with great care and conscientiousness, at least in so far as white jurors are concerned. It seems somewhat singular that in a county containing 10,000 Negroes his eyes never fell upon an honest, sober, reputable and taxpaying Negro.[77]

In deciding the case the court held that the evidence and the " long, unbroken absence of Negroes from juries selected " was tantamount to discrimination against Negroes in regard to jury service. The practice followed in Maryland, reasoned the court, " which from beginning to end confined the selection to white men, excluded Negroes as effectively as if such a restriction was

---

such instances the defendant has appeal to the Supreme Court, not as a matter of right, but by certiorari, a writ of grace, which might be granted or denied at the discretion of the Court.

[75] 161 Atl. 284 (Md. Court of Appeals).

[76] *Ibid.*, 286.

[77] New York *Times*, July 12, 1932, 16.

prescribed by statute." [78] In the view of the court an unconstitutional discrimination had been committed which was sufficient cause to reverse the lower court and order a new trial.

This decision of the Maryland Court of Appeals in the *Lee* case is unique in that it represents a departure from a practice followed by both southern state courts and the United States Supreme Court in such matters. It represents an attempt to go behind the law and determine the effect of its application. Both the statute and the practice followed in Maryland in regard to the selection of jurors were, on their face, non-discriminatory; however, their operation produced a contrary result. By this decision the Maryland court took a forward step in the application of the "equal protection" clause of the Fourteenth Amendment which the United States Supreme Court consistently refused to take.

Less than eight months after the decision in the *Lee* case, a case involving the exclusion of Negroes from jury service in Virginia gained wide attention. This case, *Hale v. Crawford,*[79] arose from the indictment of George Crawford, a Negro, for murder in Loudoun County, Virginia, by an all white jury. Crawford, who had escaped to Massachusetts and was ordered returned to Virginia, filed a petition for a writ of habeas corpus in the United States District Court at Boston against his return to Virginia. His plea was that Negroes were excluded from the grand jury which had indicted him in violation of the Fourteenth Amendment.

An essential difference between this case and most other jury cases should be noted. The *Crawford* case stood on the argument of the impossibility of a fair trial in jurisdictions which discriminated against Negroes in jury service. The issue of exclusion in this case was raised before the actual trial whereas in most jury cases the question was raised during trial proceedings. Walter White of the National Association for the Advancement of Colored People commented:

---

[78] 161 Atl. 288. See Henry J. McGuinn, "Equal Protection and Fair Trials in Maryland," *Journal of Negro History,*" XXIV (1939), 154–66 for a discussion of this case.

[79] 65 Fed. (2d) 739 (C.C.A. 1st Ct., Mass., 1933).

> This case involved an entirely new approach to the question of Negroes serving on juries. It differs from the Scottsboro and other cases in that these cases seek to set aside a verdict after conviction, whereas here our attorneys are attempting to establish that a State which bars Negroes from . . . jury service in violation of the Fourteenth Amendment . . . cannot demand the return of a fugitive Negro because such a State has already illegally and unconstitutionally indicted the fugitive and denied him his rights even before his actual trial.[80]

Federal Judge James A. Lowell granted the writ applied for in April, 1933. He ruled that the indictment was void on the ground that Negroes had been unconstitutionally excluded from service on the grand jury which had indicted Crawford. Commenting on the case Judge Lowell said:

> Why send this Negro back to Virginia, when I know and everyone knows that the Supreme Court will say the trial is illegal. They say justice is blind, but it is not blind as a bat. It goes against my Yankee common sense to have a case go to trial and then be thrown out.[81]

Judge Lowell was severely criticized by southern Congressmen for his decision and threatening efforts were made to impeach him.[82] On appeal to the United States Circuit Court of Appeals, Judge Lowell was reversed and Crawford was ordered returned to Virginia to stand trial. The court ruled that the question of discrimination against Negroes in regard to jury service was not

---

80 Press statement, New York *Times,* April 26, 1933, 17. See also Washington *Afro-American,* April 29, 1933, 2.

81 Quoted in *News-Week,* I (May 6, 1933), 27. This position appears to be based upon an assumption unsubstantiated by any Supreme Court ruling prior to May, 1933.

82 Representative Smith of Virginia felt that Judge Lowell's continuance upon the bench was "a menace to the peace and order of his country and to the fair and equal administration of justice." He charged him with making public expressions of contempt for members of Congress, ignoring decisions of the Supreme Court, and flaunting an order of rendition issued by the Governor of Massachusetts. A committee was appointed by the House of Representatives to investigate Judge Lowell and $5,000 was appropriated for that purpose. Washington *Afro-American,* May 6, 1933, 2; Richmond *Times-Dispatch,* June 12, 1933, 6.

open to determination in habeas corpus proceedings in a Federal court in the first instance. Evidence on the question was inadmissible; therefore, the District Court had erred in admitting such evidence and had to be reversed.[83]

The results of the *Crawford* case are not easily measured. There is some evidence that raising the constitutional question of the exclusion of Negroes from jury service in Loudoun County influenced other counties in Virginia to include Negroes on juries for the first time in many years.[84] But more than this, this case when linked with the *Lee* and *Scottsboro* cases, served to publicize the whole question of calling Negroes for jury service in southern jurisdictions.

The second *Scottsboro* case which was decided in 1935, in reality two cases, *Norris v. Alabama* [85] and *Patterson v. Alabama,*[86] marks the height of the concerted attack upon the exclusion of Negroes from jury service.[87] In 1932 the Supreme Court reversed the courts of Alabama and remanded the case for a new trial. During the second trial counsel for the Negro youths motioned to quash the trial venue on the basis of Alabama's "long continued, systematic and arbitrary exclusion of Negroes from jury service, solely because of race and color" in violation of the Fourteenth Amendment. The motion was overruled by the trial court, and the judgment of this court was later affirmed by the Supreme Court of Alabama. The case was appealed to the United States Supreme Court on writ of certiorari.[88]

Chief Justice Hughes wrote the Court's opinion which was

---

[83] 65 Fed. (2d) 743, 744.

[84] Washington *Afro-American,* November 11, 1933, 15; Walter White, "George Crawford—Symbol," *Crisis,* XLI (1934), 15; Harry A. Jones, "The Negro Before the Courts in 1932," *Crisis,* XL (1933), 230.

[85] 294 U. S. 587.

[86] *Ibid.,* 600.

[87] Frank L. Owsley, "Scottsboro, the Third Crusade," *American Review,* I (1933), 258–85, concludes that the attack on the southern jury system of the early thirties was a crusade for justice for the Negro comparable in many respects to the Abolition movement and Reconstruction. He finds that in the main the same groups—intelligentsia, industrialists, and journalists—have supported each of the three movements.

[88] 294 U. S. 587, 588.

handed down on April 1, 1935. In the opening part of the opinion, the Chief Justice indicated that the Supreme Court was prepared to take the progressive step of going behind the law which the Maryland Court of Appeals had taken three years earlier in the *Lee* case. He declared: "When a federal right is specifically set up, it is within the province of the Court to determine not merely whether it was denied in express terms but also whether it was denied in substance and effect." [89] An examination of the record revealed that no Negroes had been called for jury service in the county where the petitioner was tried for more than a generation though many were qualified to serve. This seemed to establish a *prima facie* case of unconstitutional discrimination. The Court could find "no constitutional justification for the long-continued, unvarying, and wholesale exclusion of Negroes from jury service." [90] Officials of Alabama, by not calling Negroes for service, by omitting their names from jury rolls, and by neglecting to give consideration to the qualifications of Negroes, had denied the petitioner equal protection of law in substance and effect, which contravened the Fourteenth Amendment. The "mere general assertion" by state officials that they had performed their duty in selecting jurors in a non-discriminatory manner, the opinion concluded, could not justify the complete exclusion of Negroes from jury service. The Supreme Court of Alabama was reversed a second time and the case was remanded for trial.

In the case of *Patterson v. Alabama,*[91] which was decided on the same day as *Norris v. Alabama* and in which the facts and evidence were the same, counsel for Alabama contended that the Supreme Court lacked jurisdiction in that a question of state appellate procedure rather than a federal question was involved. Admitting the duty of the Supreme Court to give proper regard to the state court's rulings in regard to its appellate procedure,

---

[89] *Ibid.,* 590.

[90] *Ibid.,* 597.

[91] *Ibid.,* 600. The single difference between the two cases was that in the Patterson trial before the court in Alabama counsel had filed a bill of exceptions later than in the *Norris* case. The Supreme Court of Alabama refused to review the case because time limitations had not been observed.

Chief Justice Hughes declared: " We cannot ignore the exceptional features of this present case." It would be anomalous, he pointed out, to reverse one decision and affirm the other in view of the fact that they differed only in the technical matter of state appellate procedure. Since the Supreme Court in the exercise of its appellate jurisdiction has " power not only to correct error in the judgment under review but to make such disposition of the case as justice requires," judgment in the *Patterson* case was " vacated " and the case was remanded to the courts of Alabama for retrial.[92]

Opinions as to the effect and significance of the *Scottsboro* decision were multitudinous, varied, and exaggerated in tone. Undoubtedly, the national publicity given this case had served to impress its importance upon the nation and to mark it as of determining value in the solution of the problem of equal justice for the Negro population of the South. There is little wonder that the United States Supreme Court was highly commended for having written " a new Bill of Rights for American Negroes " and thereby revealing that its " love of justice extends to the smallest as well as the greatest." [93] Long range results of the decision were predicted as an improvement in the civil status of Negroes in respect to rights other than that of jury service [94] and improved race relations in the South.[95]

An examination of newspaper opinion, Negro and white, leaves no doubt that immediate and fundamental changes in the legal status of the Negro in the South were expected to follow the Supreme Court's ruling in the second *Scottsboro* case. The first and most significant result expected was a revolution in the southern jury system marking the end of the " lily-white " jury and the general inclusion of Negroes on jury panels. Such a change in the jury system, it was hoped, would be an expression

---

[92] 294 U. S. 607. On retrial, all of the " Scottsboro boys " received long sentences; however, all but two were ultimately released.

[93] Norfolk *Journal and Guide,* April 6, 1935, 1; New York *Times,* April 2, 1935, 20; Washington *Post,* April 3, 1935, 8.

[94] Scovel Richardson, " Changing Concepts of the Supreme Court as They Affect the Legal Status of Negroes," 1 *National Bar Journal* 117.

[95] *Negro Year-Book,* 1937–1938, 119.

of the South's recognition of the constitutional rights of Negroes, and, therefore, something more than a mere expedient for complying with the law.[96]

More sober and realistic opinion was slow to express hope for any immediate, practical, or far-reaching results of the Supreme Court's mandate against the exclusion of Negroes from jury service. Admitting that the decision "will do the Negro no harm," one Negro writer expressed the opinion that the decision merely necessitated that the South alter its techniques of barring Negroes from participation in the administration of justice in the South.[97] Another writer declared: "Whether or not Negroes sit on juries in the South will not seriously affect our future."[98] Thus, he concluded that the decision meant practically nothing to the Negro. Any expectation of a substantial alteration in the "unofficial legal status" of Negroes as a result of the *Scottsboro* decision, some thought, "would be to disregard social realities."[99]

The immediate effect of the decision upon the South was to evoke expressions of hostility and suggestions that new subterfuges[100] would be employed to effect the exclusion of Negroes

[96] Richmond *Times-Dispatch,* April 3, 1935, 8; Washington *Afro-American,* November 9, 1935, 14. During the seven months following the decision in the second *Scottsboro* case, there is evidence that some southern jurisdictions, which had before completely ignored Negroes in making up jury rolls, began to include the names of qualified Negroes on jury lists and to call an occasional Negro to jury service. The number of jurisdictions where such a practice was begun by November, 1935, is estimated at twenty-seven. See Washington *Afro-American,* November 9, 1935, 14; Norfolk *Journal and Guide,* April 13, 1935, 1, 10; August 3, 1935, 1; August 17, 1935, 1.

[97] William Pickens, "The Supreme Court Blesses and Damns," Norfolk *Journal and Guide,* April 13, 1935, 8.

[98] Editorial by Gordon Hancock, Norfolk *Journal and Guide,* May 25, 1935, 8.

[99] 35 *Columbia Law Review,* 778; William L. Eckhardt, "The Exclusion of Negroes from Jury Service," 24 *Illinois Bar Journal,* 234, 235.

[100] A bill to limit jury service to qualified voters, and thereby reduce the number of Negroes eligible for jury service, was introduced in the Senate of Alabama on April 30, 1935. Birmingham *News,* April 30, 1935, 1. The legislature of North Carolina enacted a statute which increased the number of peremptory challenges against jurors from four to six hoping thereby to challenge successfully Negroes whose names were drawn for jury service.

from jury service. The press of Charleston, South Carolina, was most outspoken of all in this respect. One newspaper held that mixed juries were out of the question in South Carolina; therefore, the decision of the Supreme Court " can and will be evaded in South Carolina." That such a position would violate the spirit of the Fourteenth Amendment was inconsequential; since the amendment had been forced upon the South, " it is not binding upon its honor or morals." [101]

Attorneys and legal officers of southern states expressed little alarm over the decision. They held that it would result in no revolutionary change; at best it would force the occasional calling of a Negro to jury service to effectuate " technical conformity to the principle " enunciated by the Supreme Court.[102] One attorney summed up the effects of the second *Scottsboro* decision as follows:

> In reality the decision offered no basis for alarm among the white population of the southern states. Only by the force of the grossest misinterpretation can they [the effects] be imagined to constitute any danger to our present court system, and they certainly offer no grounds for fear of Negro domination of our courts, or for promiscuous jury service by Negroes. . . . An occasional Negro will sit on a grand jury. One or two will be called on a trial venire from time to time and will then be excused for cause or challenged peremptorily.[103]

Norfolk *Journal and Guide,* May 25, 1935, 8; New York *Times,* April 7, 1935, IV, 6.

[101] *News and Courier,* April 13, 1935, 4. The decision was attributed to the influences of the New Deal which complicated the race problem with " legalistic reasoners " and " slushy sentimentalists." See issue for April 4, 1935, 4. Governor Graves of Alabama declared: " Alabama is going to observe the supreme law of the land." He sent a circular letter to all the circuit judges and solicitors in Alabama ordering a revision of jury lists in instances where the names of Negroes had not been included. New York *Times,* April 5, 1935, 1.

[102] Birmingham *News,* April 5, 1935, 8; Norfolk *Journal and Guide,* April 13, 1935, 8.

[103] J. F. Barbour, " The Exclusion of Negroes from Jury Service," 8 *Mississippi Law Journal,* 196, 201.

Without doubt time has proven the opinions of this latter group most accurate. Such changes in jury practices as did occur in the years immediately following the decision have been all but imperceptible.

Six weeks after the decision in the second *Scottsboro* case was handed down, its rule was applied in a somewhat similar case arising in Oklahoma. A Negro on trial for rape challenged the trial jury on the grounds of the exclusion of Negroes from jury service solely because of race and color. After the challenge was overruled by the trial court and the state Criminal Court of Appeals had sustained this action, the United States Supreme Court granted a writ of certiorari to review the case. A *per curiam* decision was handed down by the Court on May 13, 1935, applying the rule of *Norris v. Alabama.*[104]

It cannot be asserted that the movement of 1931–1935 to enforce the application of the Fourteenth Amendment in regard to the exclusion of Negroes from jury service was entirely successful. From a legal and theoretical point of view some gain was registered; the Supreme Court had in principle broadened its application of the amendment in regard to the jury issue. Moreover, the Court had indicated a tendency to examine the evidence for itself and to inquire more thoroughly into allegations of unconstitutional discrimination. This represented an encouraging departure from the practices of the Court on this question which had been followed for more than forty years. However, in terms of practical results, the success of the movement is not yet fully demonstrated. The hesitancy, even refusal in some instances, of southern jurisdictions to comply with the mandate of the Supreme Court on the jury issue but suggests "the extent of the gap between judicially determined constitutional theorems and the practicalities of a southern judicial machinery dominated by whites." [105]

---

[104] *Hollins v. State of Oklahoma,* 295 U. S. 394. See also Washington *Afro-American,* May 11, 1935, 14. For opinion as to the effects of this decision upon the jury system in Oklahoma, see Tulsa *Daily World,* May 14, 1935, 9.

[105] 35 *Columbia Law Review,* 777.

Suffrage: The White Primary

Discrimination against Negroes in the exercise of the suffrage in the South, though constituting a political rather than a judicial problem, is not entirely unrelated to the jury issue. Both forms of discrimination were the product of the same group of race attitudes, both were practiced in the same locality, and both represented pernicious evasions or violations of equal protection of law as guaranteed by the Fourteenth Amendment. To a great extent, lack of the ballot fostered and permitted the continuation of such judicial abuses as those observed in the jury issue.

Writing on Negro suffrage in 1918, a competent scholar concluded that: "Until the Negro develops the honest, deep desire to vote and is willing to assert himself and take the power which the law holds out to him, his cause . . . is almost hopeless." [106] By 1931 it appears that Negroes, too, realized this, for there were numerous indications that protest over this disfranchisement in southern states would be intensified. Despite the social and economic changes which had taken place in the South by 1930 and the ruling of the Supreme Court in the first *Texas Primary* case, there was no appreciable increase in the number of Negro voters in the South.[107] There was a noticeable economic and educational advancement among southern Negroes, factors which under normal circumstances would result in increased political activity for a group, but these failed to register any result in terms of the enfranchisement of southern Negroes. Occasional liberal opinion in the South urged that "since the necessity for maintaining a strictly white man's party" no longer existed, politicians should stop appealing to race hatred and qualified Negroes should be permitted to vote.[108] However, in the main, public sentiment

---

[106] Kirk Porter, *A History of Suffrage in the United States,* 257.

[107] Paul Lewinson, *Race, Class and Party,* 105, holds that Negroes did not vote in representative numbers in the South in 1930 and that "there were many fewer [Negro voters] than an Abolitionist might hope, but rather more than even Southerners expected." Another author estimated that less than 250,000 Negroes voted in the eleven southern states during the six year period 1938–1944. Myrdal, *op. cit.,* I, 487–88.

[108] *Arkansas Democrat* (Little Rock), June 26, 1934, 6; Lewinson, *op. cit.,* 132–38.

appeared as much opposed to the participation of Negroes in southern politics in any considerable numbers in 1931 as it had a decade before;[109] and politicians continued to exploit the race issue.

Organized Negro protest against disfranchisement in the South resulted in two cases before the Supreme Court between 1931 and 1935 involving the white primary. The decision in the case of *Nixon v. Herndon,*[110] in 1927, had held that a state may not exclude a person from participation in a primary election solely on the basis of race or color. But the effect of the decision, as far as the participation of Negroes in the Democratic primary in Texas was concerned, was less favorable than most Negroes had anticipated. Immediately after the Supreme Court decision, the legislature of Texas enacted a new statute empowering the state executive committees of political parties to fix qualifications for participants in its primaries. A resolution was adopted by the State Executive Committee of the Democratic party, acting under authority of the new statute, limiting voters in its primaries to white Democrats. Both the statute and the resolution were upheld by the courts of Texas as non-violative of the Fourteenth Amendment.[111]

The question of the constitutionality of the Texas enactment of 1927 was presented to the Supreme Court in the case of *Nixon v. Condon,*[112] in 1932, by Dr. L. A. Nixon of El Paso, Texas, who had also carried the Texas statute of 1923 before the Court. Subsequent to the Court's ruling in *Nixon v. Herndon,* Nixon presented himself at the polls and was refused a ballot to vote in a Democratic primary. The refusal was based upon the resolution adopted by the State Executive Committee of the Democratic party limiting participation in party primaries to white Demo-

---

[109] Rayford W. Logan, *The Attitude of the Southern Press Toward Negro Suffrage, 1932–1940* (Washington, D. C., 1940), 3, 10; Lewinson, *op. cit.,* 132.

[110] *Supra,* 38–39.

[111] *Grigsby v. Harris,* 27 Fed. (2d) 942 (D.C.S.D. Tex., 1928); *White v. Lubbock,* 30 S. W. (2d) 722 (Tex., 1930).

[112] 286 U. S. 73. Both of the *Nixon* cases were financed through the state courts and the United States Supreme Court by the National Association for the Advancement of Colored People.

crats. Nixon's suit for damages was dismissed in the United States District Court, and this decree was affirmed by the United States Circuit Court.[113] The case was appealed to the Supreme Court.

Counsel for Nixon argued that the action of the election judge in denying Nixon the right to vote at the primary was entirely dependent upon the force of the statute enacted by Texas in 1927. This act had empowered the Democratic State Executive Committee to exclude Negroes from participation in Democratic primaries. In so excluding Negroes, the Committee had acted under this statutory power rather than under any inherent power it might have possessed. Therefore, both the statute and the resolution were invalid in that they authorized a classification based on color which was forbidden by the Fourteenth Amendment. Under the enactment of 1927, it was charged, the party Executive Committee had become an agent of the state and subject to legislative control; and it was impossible for the state to accomplish through an agent that which it was incompetent to accomplish in its own name.[114] Counsel for Condon, the election judge, contended that parties were voluntary associations of a private nature and, therefore, not subject to the limitations of the Fourteenth Amendment. Moreover, the statute of 1927 did not grant power to the Committee; it represented the state's withdrawal from an unlawful interference with the right of a political party to fix the qualifications of its members.

Mr. Justice Cardozo wrote the majority opinion which was read on May 2, 1932.[115] He observed that Nixon's situation was the same as when he had first appeared before the Court in 1926; he was still barred from the primary solely on the basis of color. Thus, it seemed that "identity of result has been attained through essential diversity of method." The issue to be decided upon was whether or not the legislative enactment of 1927 made political

---

[113] 34 Fed. (2d) 464; 49 Fed. (2d) 1012.

[114] 286 U. S. 75.

[115] It seems interesting that this opinion was written by the Justice who filled the place on the Supreme Court bench left vacant by the retirement of Justice Holmes. Justice Holmes had written the opinion in the case of *Nixon v. Herndon,* in 1927, which had invalidated the Texas statute of 1923.

parties instrumentalities of the state in Texas. This question the Court refused to answer categorically; however, it pointed out that the statute in question "attempts to confide authority to the Committee as to membership and to make it speak for the party as a whole."[116] Such inherent power as political parties did possess to determine their membership resided in the state convention, thought Cardozo, and could not be exercised by the party executive committee unless delegated to it by the convention.

It was obvious that the power exercised by the Democratic State Executive Committee had not been delegated by the party convention. Its source was in the conferring of power by the state rather than in the delegation of power by the party convention. The Committee had acted, therefore, "not as delegates of the party, but as delegates of the State." Justice Cardozo held that:

> When those agencies [committees] are invested with an authority independent of the will of the association in whose name they undertake to speak, they become to that extent agencies of the State itself. . . . They are not acting in matters of purely private concern.[117]

Having determined that the Democratic party in Texas was an agency of the state, Justice Cardozo stated the reasoning the Court had followed in reaching this conclusion and which would be applied in future consideration of the question. He stated:

> Whether in a given instance parties or committees are government agencies within the meaning of the Fourteenth or Fifteenth Amendments is a question the Supreme Court must determine for itself. . . . The test is not the test of being a representative of the State in the strict sense, but whether they can be classified as representatives of the State to such an extent and in such a sense that the great restraints of the Constitution set limits to their actions.[118]

---

116 286 U. S. 85.

117 *Ibid.*

118 *Ibid.*, 89.

It was not difficult to see that the Democratic State Executive Committee in Texas, as "delegates of the State's power," had carried out its official function in such a manner as to "discriminate invidiously between white citizens and black." This action violated the guarantees of equal protection of law as set forth in the Fourteenth Amendment and demanded a reversal of the judgment of the lower court which had sustained the action.

Four Justices dissented from the majority opinion in a minority opinion written by Mr. Justice McReynolds.[119] In their opinion no discriminatory results could be charged to the Texas statute of 1927. The conclusion that the Committee was an agency of the state was unsound, for the state habitually acts through "duly qualified officers and not through the representatives of mere voluntary associations." [120] For these reasons the minority held that the statute and resolution in question should have been upheld by the Court.

Statements as to the results expected to follow the decision in *Nixon v. Condon* indicate that Negroes and whites expected widely different outcomes. Negroes considered the decision the final step in their effort to secure participation in the white primary in Texas.[121] But they were not unaware that state-wide unity of Negroes in Texas was necessary if the State or County

---

[119] Justices Sutherland, Van Devanter, and Butler were the three Justices concurring in McReynolds' dissent. Though all four of them were on the bench in 1927 when the first *Texas Primary* case was decided, none had dissented.

[120] 286 U. S. 89. The fact that this was a five to four decision led an editor of the Dallas *Daily News,* May 4, 1932, II, 2, to feel that the decision "turned chiefly upon the fact that he [Cardozo] happened to be on the Court in place of the man whose place he took." This editor speculated that if Justice Holmes had been on the bench at the time the case was decided, despite his views in the first *Texas Primary* case, he "would have held if the grant of authority, by the State to the party, be void while the authority pre-existed in the party, then the grant ought to be treated as declaratory surplusage which had no effect one way or the other." In view of Justice Holmes' expressions in earlier cases involving discriminatory treatment of Negroes, it is difficult to accept this speculation as sound.

[121] Robert W. Hainsworth, "The Negro and the Texas Primaries," *Journal of Negro History,* XVIII (1933), 430.

Democratic convention was to be prevented from taking the step of hurriedly enacting a resolution limiting participation in the Democratic primary to white Democrats.[122] In his opinion Justice Cardozo seemed to indicate, in an indirect manner, that such action by the party convention would not contravene the Fourteenth Amendment.

Democratic party leaders in Texas were momentarily confused as to what action to take. One resignedly suggested extending permission to Negroes to vote in party primaries, but in separate lines.[123] "Discrimination against them," some urged, "is not useful; it is not reasonable; it is not even expedient." [124] Others, denouncing the Supreme Court decision as "about as close to the line of arbitrariness as any decision ever handed down by the Supreme Court," predicted that the decision would have little effect on political matters in Texas.[125] It was estimated that less than 10,000 Negroes would make an attempt to avail themselves of the opportunity to vote in the Democratic primary.[126]

The majority opinion among Democrats in Texas, however, was that some immediate action be taken to bar Negroes from the party primary which would successfully circumvent the Supreme Court's decision.[127] Most acceptable of the suggestions advanced to accomplish this end was the adoption of a resolution by the state party convention limiting membership in the Democratic party and participation in its primaries to white citizens of the state. This action was taken on May 24, 1932,

---

122 San Antonio *Express,* May 4, 1932, 2, 5.

123 Hainsworth, *loc. cit.,* 431.

124 Editorial, Dallas *Morning News,* May 4, 1932, II, 2. This editorial held that the Negroes, who would vote the Democratic ticket in Texas if the discriminatory bar were let down, should not be feared either for their numbers or for their attitude toward citizenship and law.

125 Galveston *Daily News,* May 4, 1932, 4; Houston *Post,* May 4, 1932, 2.

126 Houston *Post,* May 4, 1932, 2.

127 On June 21, 1932, Mayor C. M. Chambers of San Antonio threatened that if Texas politicians continued their attempts to evade the decision of the Supreme Court, he would submit a resolution to the National Democratic Convention, soon to convene, "inviting all persons regardless of race or color to participate in all elections." San Antonio *Express,* June 21, 1932, 4.

three weeks after the Supreme Court had handed down its decision in the case of *Nixon v. Condon.*[128]

Negroes in Texas immediately initiated action questioning the constitutionality of the action of the Democratic state party convention in excluding them from the primaries. The result was that, between May 24, 1932 and April 1, 1935, the contest over the Texas primary issue was largely confined to the state and Federal courts in Texas. Three cases were the product of this phase of the controversy. Two of these cases were decided in Federal District Courts and the other in a state appellate court; and the net results of the litigation were conflicting applications of the rule established by the Supreme Court in *Nixon v. Condon.* These three cases represent an effort to prevent the enforcement of the party resolution by mandamus and injunction.

In the first of these cases,[129] Julius White, a Negro, sought a writ of mandamus in the United States District Court for the Eastern District of Texas. He desired an order to compel the Harris County Democratic Committee to instruct the election judge to allow him to vote in a forthcoming primary election. Counsel for White contended that the resolution adopted by the state convention on May 24, 1932, and the subsequent action of the County Committee declaring the resolution valid in Harris County, deprived White of his legal right to vote, solely on the ground of color, in violation of the Fourteenth Amendment. The court upheld this contention, reasoning that the power exercised by the state convention in adopting the resolution in question was derived from the state. This being the case, the resolution was invalid under the rule of *Nixon v. Condon.* Acts seeking to prevent White from voting in the forthcoming primary election, "because he is a Negro," were held unlawful. The opinion continued:

> For twenty-five years the Democratic party in Texas has accepted grants of power from the State and sur-

[128] John B. Chamberlin, "The Validity of Texas Legislation Limiting Voting at Primaries," 27 *Illinois Law Review,* 688; Houston *Post,* May 4, 1932, 2.

[129] *White v. County Dem. Comm. of Harris County,* 60 Fed. (2d) 973 (1932).

> rendered its own inherent powers until the party has little or no discretion in the management of party affairs. . . . The Democratic party in Texas has chosen to be known as a child and agency of the State of Texas.[130]

Having decided that the action of the state convention was unconstitutional, it was still necessary to determine whether or not the complainant was entitled to the relief sought—a writ of mandamus. The court found that while it had jurisdiction over both the parties concerned and the subject-matter under litigation, it was without the power to grant a writ of mandamus.[131] The case was dismissed for want of jurisdiction.

Less than ten days after the decision in this case, the Court of Civil Appeals of Texas was confronted with the question of the constitutionality of the party resolution barring Negroes from Democratic primaries in Texas. This was the case of *County Democratic Committee in Bexar County v. Booker*.[132] While the facts in the two cases are very similar, this case differed from the *White* case in that it sought to prevent enforcement of the resolution in question by injunction rather than by mandamus. Injunctive relief had been granted by the lower court on the grounds that Booker, the Negro complainant, would be unlawfully deprived of his right to vote if the resolution were enforced. However, on appeal by the County Committee, the appellate court reversed the lower court and dismissed the suit for injunction holding that the rule of *Nixon v. Condon* did not apply. In the opinion of the court, the resolution was the " free voluntary act expressing the will of the Democratic party in Texas "; and as a voluntary political association, the Democratic party was free to determine who shall be members and who shall participate in its primaries.[133]

The decision in the *Booker* case was a divided one with Judge Cobb dissenting. In his minority opinion he declared: " In view of Supreme Court decisions and our primary laws . . . the state

[130] *Ibid.*, 974.

[131] *Ibid.*, 975. See also Chamberlin, *loc. cit.*, 688; 6 *Southern California Law Review*, 173.

[132] 53 S. W. (2d) 123 (1932).

[331] *Ibid.*, 125.

executive committee, the state convention, and each of the appellants [members of the County Committee] are to be classified as representatives of the State." [134] As representatives of the state, their actions were limited by the prohibitions of the Fourteenth Amendment. Judge Cobb was inclined to believe that the majority had been led to a faulty conclusion through its failure to consider two essential facts: that primary elections in Texas were financed in part by the state; and that the Democratic State Executive Committee, already defined as a state agency by the Supreme Court, declared the resolution of the convention valid and certified it to the County Chairmen.[135] These considerations should have led the court to a different result.

Efforts to secure injunctive relief against the enforcement of the resolution having failed in the state court, an attempt was made to obtain it from the United States District Court for the Southern District of Texas.[136] In January, 1933, W. M. Drake, a Negro, sought to restrain the Democratic Executive Committee of Houston from depriving him of his right to vote in a Democratic primary to be held on January 28th. He urged that such a deprivation would contravene the "equal protection" clause of the Fourteenth Amendment. Denying the contention of the plaintiff that the Committee was a state agency, the court held that the Committee was acting under "the inherent powers of the party." In excluding Drake from the primary, it violated none of his rights as protected by the Fourteenth Amendment.

The decision in the *Drake* case left the question of the validity of the resolution of the Democratic state convention excluding Negroes from party primaries in a confused state. In one instance, the *White* case, a United States District Court had ruled this action a violation of the Fourteenth Amendment; in another, the *Booker* case, a state appellate court had upheld the action; and in still another, the *Drake* case, a second United States District Court had ruled the action constitutional. Such a confused state of affairs made it imperative that an early and clarifying

[134] *Ibid.*, 126.

[135] *Ibid.*

[136] *Drake v. Exec. Comm. of the Dem. Party of Houston*, 2 Fed. Supp. 486.

ruling on the question be obtained from the United States Supreme Court.

On April 1, 1935, the Supreme Court had an opportunity to consider the question of the validity of the resolution in the case of *Grovey v. Townsend.*[137] The case arose from the fact that Grovey, a Negro resident of Harris County, Texas, was refused a ballot to vote in a Democratic primary by the County Clerk on the basis of the resolution of the Democratic state convention of May 24, 1932. Counsel for Grovey advanced the following contentions for consideration by the Court:

1. A state officer in refusing to furnish a ballot in obedience to the laws of Texas and the subsequent denial of the right to vote was state action.
2. The resolution of the state convention limiting membership to whites doesn't relieve the exclusion of Negroes from participation in Democratic primary elections of its true character as the act of the state, since the primary was wholly statutory in origin and held under state compulsion.
3. As a Negro couldn't be denied a ballot at a general election on account of race or color, if exclusion from the primary renders his vote at the general election insignificant and useless, the result is to deny him the suffrage altogether.[138]

The opinion of the Court was written by Mr. Justice Roberts. He first called attention to the fact that the case under consideration was substantially different from the case of *Nixon v. Condon* which was relied upon by the petitioner. In the case before the Court the qualifications for voting in the party primary were "established by the party represented in convention" while in the

[137] 295 U. S. 45. It is to be noted that this decision, unfavorable to the Negro interest involved, was handed down on April 1, 1935. This was the same day that the decision in the second *Scottsboro* case, a decision favorable to the Negro interest involved, was handed down. This coincidence led William Pickens in "The Supreme Court Blesses and Damns," Norfolk *Journal and Guide,* April 13, 1935, 8, to remark: "If one were suspicious of the Court's motives, it would look as if they had made a trade . . . as an apology to the race's enemies for the Scottsboro decision."

[138] 295 U. S. 48–55, *passim.*

earlier case, qualifications had been established by the party Executive Committee. The action of the party convention "upon its face is not state action," declared the Court. This pronouncement seemed to dispose of the petitioner's first contention.

There was little sound reasoning in the second contention advanced by the petitioner, thought Justice Roberts. He had failed to distinguish between statutory provisions for the expression of party preference and state regulation "to protect the suffrage of members of organizations against fraud," on the one hand, and the unconstitutional statutory grant of powers of exclusion on the other. Admitting that a state legislature is without power to limit or determine the membership of a political party, the Court held that once parties were formed "the state may legislate for their governance." This being true, it was a logical conclusion that state officers, acting under the mandate of the state party convention in respect to the "eligibility to participate in the party's deliberations," were acting under authority of the party, not the state.[139] Concluding that "in Texas the state convention of a party has [not] become a mere instrumentality or agency for expressing the voice or will of the state," [140] the Court held that the petitioner had been denied no constitutional right in pursuance to state mandate.[141]

Expressions of opinion among Negroes in regard to the decision in *Grovey v. Townsend* revealed a note of keen disappointment. Perhaps this was to be expected from a purely racial point of view and in view of the Supreme Court's position in

---

[139] *Ibid.*, 53.

[140] *Ibid.*, 54.

[141] While the question of the Texas primary was before the Court, a case was brought before the United States Circuit Court in New Orleans invoking the Fourteenth Amendment against the Louisiana "understanding Clause." In this case Trudeau, a Negro, held that this clause of the Louisiana constitution, which established the ability to read and interpret any clause of the state constitution or of the Constitution of the United States as a qualification for voting, denied him equal protection of the law. The clause in question "lays down one test," declared the court, "which applies uniformly and without discrimination to voters of every race or color." Thus, the "understanding clause" was upheld. See *Trudeau v. Bonds*, 65 Fed. (2d) 564 (1933).

the two earlier *Texas Primary* cases. The decision was regarded as "regrettable, both from a racial and a political viewpoint," for its result would be to "disfranchise Negroes in so far as the real exercise of the suffrage is concerned." [142] By sanctioning a "subterfuge" the Supreme Court had relegated the problem of Negro suffrage to the status of a local question and subjected it to local control. It was generally felt that the decision settled, with a great deal of finality, the question of the participation of Negroes in the Texas primary.[143] The decision left a marked advantage to the ingenuity of Texas Democrats.

Litigation by Negroes between 1931 and 1935, invoking the Fourteenth Amendment against southern disfranchisement devices, appears to have fallen far short of its goal. However, the cases on the subject do reveal the numerous methods which might be employed successfully to circumvent the limitations of the Fourteenth Amendment. The apparent failure of court action as a means of effectuating the enfranchisement of southern Negroes led to the consideration of alternatives to accomplish the same end. Prominent among the alternatives suggested was a dual program of education which emphasized civic consciousness and responsibility on the part of the Negro and an understanding of American democracy and democratic practices on the part of whites.[144] During the late thirties there was no significant legal

---

[142] Norfolk *Journal and Guide,* April 13, 1935, 8. See also Ralph J. Bunche, "Tactics and Problems of Minority Groups," *Journal of Negro Education,* IV (1935), 319.

[143] E. Franklin Frazier, "The Negro in the American Social Order," *Journal of Negro Education,* IV (1935), 302, stated that the *Grovey v. Townsend* decision "indicates that the path to political power through the white primary offers no promise to disfranchised blacks." Another writer, P. Bernard Young, Norfolk *Journal and Guide,* April 13, 1935, 10, seemed to predict a future change in the Supreme Court's position on the Texas primary question. He wrote: "The Texas barrier will not be effective long. The Court in 1935 didn't ferret out the trickery behind the statutes. Later, it will go behind the law." Eight years after the *Grovey* case, when the personnel of the Court had greatly changed, in the case of *Smith v. Allwright,* 321 U. S. 649 (1944), the Court reversed the *Grovey* decision. In this instance the exclusion of Negroes from the Democratic primary in Texas was held to violate the Fifteenth Amendment.

[144] Mangum, *op. cit.,* 424. American interracial organizations and national

action on the part of Negroes to force the enfranchisement of Negroes under the guarantees of the Fourteenth Amendment.

While national attention was focused upon the issues of fair trials for Negroes and the participation of Negroes in the white primary, the old constitutional issue of residential segregation by legislative enactment was temporarily revived. This issue had been frequently litigated between 1920 and 1930; but it had lain dormant since the Supreme Court's ruling in the case of *City of Richmond v. Deans* in 1930. The issue was revived by Oklahoma City in 1933.

Governor Murray of Oklahoma declared a state of martial law to exist in Oklahoma City because of rioting and bloodshed which was threatening as the result of the establishment of residences by Negroes in white neighborhoods. Acting under his emergency military powers, he established segregated residential zones for Negroes and whites with a "non-trespass" zone between the two. Martial law was to be maintained until the city enacted a valid segregation ordinance.[145] The City Council enacted an ordinance which was identical in many respects with those already held unconstitutional by the Supreme Court between 1920 and 1930; the essential difference in this instance was that the ordinance was supported by valid military powers of the Governor.[146]

An action brought by a Negro to prevent the enforcement of the ordinance resulted in its invalidation by the Supreme Court of Oklahoma in 1935. This tribunal felt that, in view of the ruling in *Buchanan v. Warley* and the action of the Supreme Court in repeatedly refusing to sustain similar ordinances, the question of the validity of segregation ordinances was no longer open to debate. No matter what the beliefs, hopes, or desires

---

Negro sororities and fraternities made valuable contributions to this program of education.

[145] Mangum, *op. cit.*, 145; *Jones v. Oklahoma City,* 78 Fed. (2d) 860 (C.C.A. 10th. Ct., 1935); *Allen v. City of Oklahoma,* 52 Pac. (2d) 1058 (Okla., 1935).

[146] The editor of the *Daily Oklahoman* was more farsighted than either the Governor or the City Council. He contended that the best approach to the problem growing out of "residence" was, not official action of the kind taken, but the formation of a non-official, bi-racial commission to consider the problem. See *Daily Oklahoman* (Oklahoma City), November 27, 1935, 8.

of persons on the subject of residential segregation might be, the court had no choice but to determine rights and liberties under law and to enforce the same when determined. In the face of a "final, binding and conclusive" adjudication on the subject, declared the court, "our views on race problems are entirely beside the question." [147] The city authorities were severely criticized for their action.

> The City Council of Oklahoma City had before it the decision of the Supreme Court of the United States in the Warley case when it enacted the present ordinance. The city authorities well knew, or should have known, that its action was futile and in disregard of the decision of the highest and final authority in the United States upon the subject.[148]

The contention that the ordinance was valid as a means of causing the withdrawal of the Governor's martial law decree was untenable in the view of the court. "The exercise of wrongful police power to defeat illegal martial law is police power wrongfully employed," reasoned the court.[149] There was no recourse but to reverse the lower court's ruling of validity and remand the case for grant of injunctive relief against enforcement.[150] Except for the unsuccessful attempt of Winston Salem, North Carolina, in 1941,[151] the Oklahoma City ordinance represented the final attempt to effectuate residential segregation by legislative enactment.

While the number of cases won and lost is far from a reliable indication of the extent of enjoyment of a constitutional right, an analysis of the number, distribution, and final disposition of cases sometimes suggests significant tendencies. This appears to be true in regard to cases involving the Fourteenth Amendment and the Negro between 1931 and 1935. According to the num-

---

[147] *Allen v. City of Oklahoma,* 52 Pac. (2d) 1057.

[148] *Ibid.,* 1058.

[149] *Ibid.*

[150] Two similar cases arising in Oklahoma City, *Scott v. Watt* and *Ex parte Lee,* 52 Pac. (2d) 1059 (1935), were likewise decided under the rule of *Buchanan v. Warley.*

[151] *Clinard v. City of Winston Salem,* 6 S. E. (2d) 867.

ber of cases, it appears that Negroes invoked the guarantees of the Fourteenth Amendment more frequently during the period 1931–1935 than during the period 1920–1930. During the latter period of eleven years there were eighteen cases as compared with nineteen cases for the former period of five years. Of the nineteen cases decided between 1931 and 1935, final decisions were rendered in the United States Supreme Court in seven instances; [152] in United States Circuit Courts of Appeal in four instances; and in state appellate courts in six instances. Seventeen of the total number of cases were decided at the appellate level during this period as compared with thirteen of eighteen cases for the earlier period. Decisions favorable to the Negro interest involved were handed down in eleven of nineteen cases. It seems impressive that only one of the seven decisions handed down by the Supreme Court, of the character under discussion, was unfavorable to the Negro interest involved.[153]

These statistics indicate a tendency toward a more liberal interpretation and application of the Fourteenth Amendment in cases involving the Negro before both state [154] and Federal courts. Changes in both personnel and practices on the part of the United States Supreme Court tended to incline the Court toward a more liberal point of view than it had hitherto held. There was some expression of conviction as early as 1931 that the Supreme Court was inclined toward the liberal view.[155] " For the first time in its history," observed one writer, " a definite trend toward liberalism " was apparent. Moreover, it was notable that:

---

[152] See Appendix.

[153] *Grovey v. Townsend,* 295 U. S. 45 (1935).

[154] Harry A. Jones, " The Negro Before the Courts in 1932," *Crisis,* XL (1933), 230, attributes this tendency in state courts to two factors: fear on the part of state judges of being reversed and the desire of state courts to " assure the Nation as a whole that the court will give the Negro a square deal."

[155] Joseph P. Pollard, " Our Supreme Court Goes Liberal," *Forum,* LXXXVI (1931), 193–95; Oliver McKee, " The Liberal Supreme Court," *Outlook,* LIX (1931), 171–90; Zechariah Chafee, " Liberal Trends in the Supreme Court," *Current History,* XXXV (1931), 338–44.

> . . . the Supreme Court was leaning to the liberal side at a time when social and economic unrest and stirring is significant. It prevents radicals from feeling the cards are stacked against them when they come before the court by the existence of a safely conservative court.[156]

No doubt the changes made in the personnel of the Court between 1930 and 1932 greatly influenced tendencies toward liberalism.[157] The appointment of Chief Justice Hughes and Justice Roberts in 1930 and of Justice Cardozo to succeed Justice Holmes, together with the presence on the bench of Justices Brandeis and Stone, gave the Court a liberal nucleus which usually stood together.[158] Public interest in the appointment of liberally inclined Justices was manifest in the contest over the confirmation of Circuit Judge John J. Parker of North Carolina as Justice of the Supreme Court. Confirmation was opposed by two major groups—the Negro and labor. Labor opposed Parker for a decision he had handed down upholding " yellow-dog " labor contracts. Negroes opposed him because of earlier public utterances which convinced them that Parker's views were inimical to the Negro's constitutional rights; and elevation to the Supreme Court would bolster the conservative majority.[159] Combined opposition

---

156 McKee, *loc. cit.*, 171.

157 Pollard, *loc. cit.*, 193, attributes the liberal tendencies in the Court to "the judicial genius of Justice Holmes and Brandeis whose forceful views which were written into the Court's records for twenty years gradually seeped into the consciousness of the American people and moulded new attitudes." On this point it can be noted that Justice Brandeis concurred in most of the decisions of the Court upholding the constitutional guarantees of equal protection and due process of law in regard to Negroes. See Washington *Afro-American,* October 11, 1941, 6.

158 Justices Van Devanter, Sutherland, Butler, and McReynolds, sometimes joined by Chief Justice Hughes, usually stood together on the conservative side of most issues. The result was that there was an unprecedentedly large number of five to four decisions handed down by the Supreme Court. See New York *Times,* April 7, 1935, VII, 17; April 9, 1935, VI, 3.

159 Paul E. Baker, *Negro-White Adjustment,* 83; Walter White, "The Negro and the Supreme Court," *Harper's Magazine,* CLXII (1931), 238-42. Negro opposition was organized and directed by the National Association for the Advancement of Colored People. For a treatment of the movement

of these two groups brought about the defeat of Parker's nomination. Parker's defeat represented the first defeated nomination for Justice of the Supreme Court in more than thirty years.[160]

Negroes were aware of the possible effects which the addition of two liberally inclined Justices to the Supreme Court might have upon litigation involving their constitutional rights. One Negro writer advised: "As far as possible, every opportunity should be asserted to have the present personnel of that Court [Supreme Court] to pass upon pressing matters of a civil nature." [161] To this writer the Supreme Court appeared to be more "fairly disposed toward colored people" than at any time in its history. Such convictions that the Negro's best chance of obtaining justice was in the new Supreme Court [162] are astonishingly different from expressions on the subject made by Negroes in the early twenties.[163] Without doubt, the conviction that the Supreme Court personnel of the period 1931–1935 was favorably inclined to the protection of the constitutional rights of minorities, was a significant factor in the acceleration of the program of court action which took place during this period.

A change in policy, as well as viewpoint, appears to have resulted from the change in the personnel of the Supreme Court during the early thirties. One of the most significant and en-

---

see W. E. B. DuBois, "Defeat of Judge Parker," *Crisis,* XXXVII (1930), 225–27; Herbert J. Seligmann, "Negroes and the Supreme Court," *Forum,* LXXXVI (1931), Supp., 24; N.A.A.C.P., *Twenty-First Annual Report,* 1930, 7–13.

[160] Cortez A. M. Ewing, *Judges of the Supreme Court, 1789–1937* Minneapolis, 1938, 17. Eleven years after the defeat of Judge Parker's nomination and exactly one year after his favorable decision in *Alston v. School Board of City of Norfolk,* 112 Fed. (2d) 992 (1940), Judge Parker was supported by an influential Negro newspaper as successor to Chief Justice Hughes. Norfolk *Journal and Guide,* June 7, 1941, 8.

[161] Harry A. Jones, *loc. cit.,* 230.

[162] Bunche, *loc. cit.,* 316–17, refutes this conclusion and holds that Negroes could expect no general relief from the Supreme Court because of the Court's acquiescence in prevailing attitudes toward the Negro.

[163] See Charles H. Wesley, "The Historical Basis of Negro Citizenship," *Opportunity,* II (1924), 359; C. G. Woodson, "Fifty Years of Negro Citizenship as Qualified by the United States Supreme Court," *Journal of Negro History,* VI (1921), 52–53.

couraging tendencies in this respect was the greater willingness of the Court to review cases involving questions of the constitutional rights of Negroes. In some situations, as for example the allegation of discriminatory treatment in jury service, the Negro had appealed to the Supreme Court, not as a matter of right, but by writ of certiorari, a writ of grace which the Court may grant or deny at its discretion. Prior to 1931 the Court granted this writ with great reluctance, especially if the question involved was loaded with sectional dynamite as was likely to be the case when an issue involved the rights of Negroes under the Fourteenth Amendment.

Between 1931 and 1935 access to the Supreme Court in most of the cases under the Fourteenth Amendment was by writ of certiorari. While the decision in *Grovey v. Townsend* was unsatisfactory, it was encouraging to hear the Court declare: "We granted certiorari because of the federal question presented, which has not been determined by this court."[164] The willingness of the Supreme Court to review cases involving Negro issues gave whatever liberal proclivities the Court possessed more meaning; access to the Court was essential in order to translate the liberal inclinations of the Court into judicial protection of constitutional rights.

During most of the twenties, the Supreme Court was criticized for its steadfast refusal to go behind the law when determining questions of the constitutionality of legislation which affected the rights of Negroes.[165] An examination of the wording and administration of such legislation was the extent of the Court's examination. It was unnecessary, the Court felt, to consider the intent of the framers or the effect of the measure in order to determine the question of constitutionality. The influence of such a procedure upon the application of the Fourteenth Amendment has been estimated as follows:

---

[164] 295 U. S. 45.

[165] Kelly Miller, "Is the Color Line Crumbling?" *Opportunity,* VII (1929), 292; Wesley, *loc. cit.,* 359. John A. Wigmore, "The Qualities of Current Judicial Decisions," 9 *Illinois Law Review,* 533, characterized such a practice as "undue servitude to the bondage of precedent."

> To be effective the Fourteenth Amendment must be given a broad interpretation which permits the Court to examine the intent as well as the particular wording of statutes. Unless the intention and effect of acts which are seemingly unconstitutional but not within the express wording of the Constitution are examined, loopholes can be devised so that almost every restriction of the Constitution will be a nullity. . . .[166]

A change of policy in regard to the examination of the intent of enactments was indicated by the Supreme Court in the case of *Nixon v. Condon* in 1932. Here the Court took the position that the mere examination of the wording of the Texas statute of 1927 was insufficient to determine its constitutionality. This position was apparent in the declaration that: "Whether in a given instance committees of parties are government agencies within the meaning of the Fourteenth and Fifteenth Amendments is a question the Supreme Court must decide for itself."[167] According to the express wording of the statute, political parties were private, voluntary associations beyond the scope of the prohibitions of the Fourteenth Amendment. However, a consideration of the intent and effect of the statute led to the conclusion that political parties were agents of the state and, therefore, subject to the limitations imposed by the amendment.[168]

Hardly less important than the tendency to consider the intent and effect of enactments, allegedly established in violation of the Fourteenth Amendment, was the increased tendency of the Supreme Court to make an independent examination of the facts in determining whether or not a constitutional right had been disregarded. One criticism made of the Court in regard to criminal cases, where Negroes charged a denial of due process or equal protection of the law, was its practice of giving conclusive effect to the state court's findings of fact. The Supreme Court refused to interfere if the state appellate court, after its examination of the facts, found no error in the ruling of the

---

166 George Ajootian, "The Right of Negroes to Vote in State Primaries," 12 *Boston University Law Review*, 694.

167 286 U. S. 89.

168 *Ibid.*

lower court.[169] This policy was explained as necessary in order to prevent a trespass by the Court upon the criminal jurisdiction of state courts and in order to prevent raising barriers against the enforcement of criminal law.[170]

Among the Supreme Court Justices who opposed this policy was Justice Holmes. He consistently urged that the Supreme Court should "cut under the record" in order to see whether or not the facts of record, as certified by the state appellate court, were different from the actual or prevailing facts.[171] This view was not adopted by the Court until its decision in the first *Scottsboro* case in 1932. In answer to Powell's charge of denial of right of counsel, the Supreme Court of Alabama examined the record and proceedings of the trial court and concluded that the charge was not substantiated by the record. According to its usual practice, the Supreme Court would have accepted the finding of the state court as conclusive. But in this case the Court examined the record for itself and came to the opposite conclusion that while "the gesture of furnishing counsel was made," the petitioner was not given counsel "in any substantial sense."[172] There was an indication given in 1935 that independent examinations of the record by the Court would prevail.[173] At this time

---

[169] Joseph Sugarman, "The Right to Counsel," 13 *Boston University Law Review*, 92–96; Felix Frankfurter, "A Notable Decision," New York *Times*, November 13, 1932, II, 1.

[170] Mr. Justice McReynolds, who dissented from the majority opinion favorable to the Negro petitioner in every criminal case in which he participated between 1920–1932, refused to follow the majority because their opinion represented an interference with the criminal jurisdiction of the states. For a full statement of Justice McReynolds' position on this question see his dissenting opinion in the following cases: *Moore v. Dempsey,* 261 U. S. 86 (1923); *Aldridge v. United States,* 283 U. S. 308 (1931); and his concurrence in the dissenting opinion of Justice Butler in *Powell v. Alabama,* 287 U. S. 46 (1932). Justice Sutherland, who concurred in McReynolds' dissenting opinion in *Moore v. Dempsey,* held the same position on the subject.

[171] Sugarman, *loc. cit.*, 98.

[172] *Powell v. Alabama,* 287 U. S. 58.

[173] Constitutional law authorities have held that independent examination of the facts by the Supreme Court tends to check arbitrary action by state courts and "demands that the elemental decencies be observed in conform-

the Supreme Court undertook an independent examination of the record in deciding the second *Scottsboro* case. The purpose of the examination, as stated by the Court, was to determine, not merely whether a constitutional right was expressly denied, but " whether it was denied in substance and effect." [174]

Tendencies such as these observed in the Supreme Court between 1931 and 1935 [175] indicate that the Court was at least inclined toward a more liberal interpretation and application of the Fourteenth Amendment than it had followed during the twenties. However, it should be borne in mind that the tendencies referred to above were mere tendencies in 1935 and not the prevailing practices of the Court.[176] But even tendencies in a liberal direction had their effect upon both the actions of state agencies and the thinking of Negroes.

State courts and legislatures realized the possibility of an examination of their actions and of the application of the rule of " substantial effect " by the Supreme Court. They tended to be more hesitant in taking action which effectuated a substantial, though not an expressed, disregard of the prohibitions laid down in the Fourteenth Amendment. This in itself might be regarded as a progressive step from the Negro's point of view; it forecast a decrease in the evasive practices of southern states, one of the most formidable barriers to the full enforcement of the Fourteenth Amendment through court action. Without doubt

---

ing with the due process of law clause." Charles B. Nutting, " The Supreme Court, the Fourteenth Amendment, and State Criminal Cases," 3 *University of Chicago Law Review,* 259; 31 *Michigan Law Review,* 253–55; Sugarman, *loc. cit.,* 98.

[174] *Norris v. Alabama,* 294 U. S. 590.

[175] In regard to the issue of discrimination against Negroes in jury service, the liberal tendencies in the Court tended to shift the burden of proof from the petitioner to the state. Absence of Negroes from juries for an extended period of time was *prima facie* evidence of discrimination which the state had to refute.

[176] Writing as late as 1935, one author remarked: " It is perhaps remarkable that more than sixty-six years after the adoption of the Fourteenth Amendment, with its operation in many directions well defined, its effectiveness in accomplishing the chief purpose of its adoption—the protection of the Negro—is still largely undecided." 20 *Michigan Law Review,* 673.

later action by Negroes in this respect found much of its inspiration in the belief that the liberal tendencies observed in the Supreme Court during this period would persist. The evidence points to the conclusion that an easier access to the Supreme Court and less hesitation by the Court in questioning the actions and conclusions of agents of southern states were the chief gains registered in the history of the Fourteenth Amendment and the Negro between 1931 and 1935.[177]

---

177 Kelly Miller, Norfolk *Journal and Guide,* May 4, 1935, 8, writing a month after the second *Scottsboro* case, expressed the conviction that Supreme Court victories resulted in mere theoretical gains for Negroes. The only practical benefit he could see from such victories was that they "keep open the door of hope to the Negro."

CHAPTER IV

ALONG NEW PATHS, 1936–1943

The intensification of a feeling of racial solidarity observed among Negroes between 1931 and 1935 and its resultant manifestations, group cooperation and protest over inequalities, tended to increase rather than diminish after 1935. Despite some evidences of liberal tendencies in the Supreme Court and the executive branch of the national government, Negroes continued to chafe under their unequal status in American society. Adroit discriminatory techniques in economic matters resulting from the depression and the advocacy of racial and religious persecution [1] in some areas seemed to threaten even the limited rights and privileges which they were permitted to exercise. The reaction of Negroes to these circumstances was the acceleration of the program of legal action to protect existing rights against further invasion and to win new ones. Since the Fourteenth Amendment had long been considered by Negroes as their "charter of liberty," this meant an increase in the number of situations and instances in which the Fourteenth Amendment would be invoked. Indeed, the period was destined to be the most prolific of all in regard to litigation by Negroes under the Fourteenth Amendment. Furthermore, legal action between 1936 and 1943 under this amendment was generally under the "equal protection" clause, thus continuing a tendency first observed during the period 1931–1935.[2] However, it is interesting to observe that the

[1] "Legislative Attempts to Eliminate Racial and Religious Persecution," 39 *Columbia Law Review,* 986.

[2] Justice Robert Jackson, a newcomer to the Supreme Court in 1941, was reported to have "rebuked" the Court for having emphasized the "equal protection" clause and neglected the "privileges and immunities" clause of the Fourteenth Amendment. Washington *Afro-American,* February 28, 1942, 4. Negroes seldom invoked the "privileges and immunities" clause because the Supreme Court, even before the turn of the century, placed a very narrow construction upon this clause and, therefore, upon the rights and privileges of citizens of the United States.

"due process" clause, infrequently appealed to between 1931 and 1935, was now invoked in a substantial number of cases.[3]

Any study of the Fourteenth Amendment and the Negro during the years 1936–1943 must take into consideration that these were the years of the New Deal. Though officially inaugurated March 4, 1933, it was perhaps only at the end of the first New Deal administration that its influences were fully felt in American life. Two basic concomitants of the New Deal—a social philosophy emphasizing the welfare of the individual and a reformed Supreme Court—appear to have exerted a profound influence upon the nature and extent of the application of the Fourteenth Amendment in matters affecting the Negro. Both of these influences have been widely controverted; however, that disagreement fails to diminish their effect upon the question of the constitutional rights of Negroes.

From the social point of view, the New Deal placed a new emphasis upon the responsibility of the Federal Government to the individual. The Federal Government was responsible for lessening the wide differences in opportunities enjoyed by its citizens and for reducing inequalities due to race and birth. The extravagant joys and fears that the New Deal "will proclaim the new social revolution . . . [and] decree that our democracy and our freedom are of more value than caste"[4] were proven ill-founded. But there was a new value placed upon the individual and his equality of opportunity which appeared to transcend consideration of both race and social status. Of great significance to Negroes was the fact that the acceptance by southern states of national benefits legislated by the New Deal compelled at least outward conformity to the doctrine of equality in distributing

---

[3] See Norfolk *Journal and Guide,* March 6, 1937, 8, and Washington *Afro-American,* March 6, 1937, 15, for a discussion of Senator Borah's proposal to alter the Fourteenth Amendment by changing the "due process" clause so as to give the states exclusive control of social and economic questions. While the proposal was inspired by the desire to prevent the use of this clause by corporations to escape state regulation, Negroes were convinced that it would "strike a death blow to human rights" and virtually repeal the basic guarantees of the Fourteenth Amendment.

[4] Editorial, Washington *Afro-American,* February 28, 1942, 1, 4.

these benefits to their citizens. To a limited extent, it meant the surrender of some discriminatory practices.[5]

A direct influence was exerted upon the question of the constitutional rights of Negroes under the Fourteenth Amendment by the "reformed Court," a secondary product of the New Deal. Defeats administered by the Supreme Court to legislative enactments implementing the New Deal economic program led to efforts to reform the Supreme Court. The allegedly "conservative" and "reactionary" attitudes which dominated the Court and invalidated New Deal legislation made it impossible for the Administration to attack economic evils in the manner desired.[6] Programs for reforming the Supreme Court were proposed which would give the Administration a safely liberal majority. While the program of statutory reform was defeated,[7] the controversy did result in opportunities for six New Deal appointments to the Supreme Court bench between 1937 and 1941.[8]

With the exception of Justices Black and Byrnes, the New Deal appointees to the Supreme Court were accepted as men of liberal views and judicial ability. They were a group of Justices, said one editor, who "write opinions with their intelligence, not with their racial prejudices."[9] Senator Black's appointment to the Supreme Court was opposed for two reasons: his lack of important legal practice and prior judicial experience and his Klan connections as reported in the press and finally admitted.[10] Furthermore, Negroes opposed the appointment because of his

[5] Gunnar Myrdal, *An American Dilemma,* II, 463 f. For an opposite view, questioning the benefit of the New Deal to Negroes, see Norfolk *Journal and Guide,* July 27, 1935, 6.

[6] Jeanette P. Nichols, *Twentieth Century United States,* 361.

[7] One opinion holds that the Supreme Court helped fight reform by adopting a more liberal attitude toward New Deal measures. Nichols, *op. cit.,* 361; Washington *Afro-American,* May 1, 1937, 18.

[8] Justices Black in 1937; Reed in 1938; Frankfurter and Douglas in 1939; Murphy in 1940; and Byrnes in 1941.

[9] Washington *Afro-American,* September 23, 1939, 4.

[10] Cortez A. M. Ewing, *Judges of the Supreme Court, 1789–1937,* 8, points out that only one of the eight men on the Court at the time of Black's appointment had ever sat on an inferior court. See also Editorial, "Hugo Black, Justice of the Supreme Court," *Opportunity,* XV (1937), 293; New York *Times,* August 13, 1937, 4, and August 15, 1937, 2.

Alabama origin. This brought concern as to Black's position in case of a question of the protection of Negroes' rights. His appointment, it was declared, would "kill the influence of the Supreme Court" due to the lack of confidence in him by minority groups, which would include Jews, Catholics, and foreigners as well as Negroes.[11] However, there was hope that, freed of the necessity of campaigning for re-election, "he would take broad views on matters involving colored citizens and other minority groups."[12] In a prophetic statement, Kelly Miller, a Negro leader, declared: "Senator Black will make a brilliant jurist whose chief concern will be social justice and safeguarding the rights and interests of all, even the humblest."[13] Objections, similar to those raised in regard to Justice Black's appointment, were raised again in regard to the appointment of the self-educated Justice Byrnes of South Carolina in 1941.

Despite their disappointment over the appointment of Justices Black and Byrnes to the Supreme Court, Negroes were satisfied that the personnel of the Court was safely liberal and would give them greater safeguards for their rights under the law than any previous Court had granted. It is to be remembered that the lack of liberal Justices on the Court had long been considered the primary difficulty in securing the full enforcement of the guarantees of the Fourteenth Amendment. The conviction that the Court was definitely liberal had a determining effect upon the Negro's legal strategy between 1936 and 1943; it fostered the plan of having the liberally constituted Court pass upon as many fundamental constitutional issues affecting the rights of Negroes as could be brought up from the lower courts. This conviction and this strategy, in great measure, help to explain the increased number of cases carried to the Supreme Court during this period which invoked the guarantees of the Fourteenth Amendment.

Equal Educational Opportunities

Efforts by Negroes to secure enforcement of the Fourteenth Amendment after 1936 tended to concentrate in two subject

[11] Washington *Afro-American,* September 25, 1937, 4.

[12] *Ibid.,* September 11, 1937, 6.

[13] *Ibid.*

areas—educational equality and fair trials in criminal cases. The question of the separate school or the classification of races in schools, first upheld in *Buntin v. United States* by a United States Circuit Court of Appeals in 1882,[14] was affirmed by the Supreme Court in *Gong Lum v. Rice* in 1927.[15] By 1935 separate schools were required by law in eighteen states and the District of Columbia;[16] these states were, with one exception, southern and border states and the race "separated" was the Negro race.[17] The separation of races for purposes of education was predicated upon the doctrine of separate but equal opportunities and facilities. However, southern attitudes had traditionally opposed wide educational opportunities for Negroes because of the fear that educational advancement of Negroes would destroy the traditional pattern of race relations in the South. These attitudes, together with conservative pronouncements by the courts, all but resulted in the vitiation of the doctrine of equality of educational opportunities as between the races.[18]

Where separate schools have been established, gross inequalities have obtained in the educational opportunities and facilities provided for Negro and white children. One author writes: "It is

[14] 10 Fed. 30.

[15] 275 U. S. 78.

[16] Doxy Wilkerson, *Special Problems of Negro Education,* Advisory Committee on Education, Staff Study No. 12 (Washington, D. C., 1939), xv. For special studies on the separate school see Maurice L. Risen, *Legal Aspects of the Separation of Races in Public Schools* (Philadelphia, 1935), 43, 48–84; Gladys T. Peterson, "The Present Status of the Negro Separate School as Defined by Court Decisions," *Journal of Negro Education,* IV (1935), 351–74.

[17] A. Bruce, "Racial Zoning by Private Contract," 21 *Illinois Law Review,* 704, holds that the doctrine of educational segregation is of northern rather than southern origin. His conclusion is based upon a decision of the Supreme Court of Massachusetts of 1849 permitting the Boston School Board to provide for the education of Negro children in separate schools. See also *Piper v. Big Pine School District of Inyo County,* 226 Pac. 926 (Calif., 1924), *Bond v. Tig Fung,* 114 So. 332 (Miss., 1922), and *Gong Lum v. Rice,* 275 U. S. 78 (1927) for instances where school laws requiring separate schools were directed at Mongolians and Indians.

[18] Paul Lewinson, *Race, Class and Party,* 35–36; Charles S. Mangum, *The Legal Status of the Negro,* 132–33; John Van Deusen, "The Negro in Politics," *Journal of Negro History,* XXVI (1936), 134.

the exception rather than the rule for Negro schools in the South to be anywhere near as efficient as those for whites. The inequalities are manifest to anyone who has even a cursory knowledge of the present status of education in the South."[19] Studies of the Negro separate school reveal that practically every aspect of the educative process was both inadequate and unequal when compared to that for whites. Thus, there was a disparity between the average annual expenditures of southern states for Negro and white children,[20] between the length of the school term,[21] and between the physical equipment provided.[22]

Court action to remove such inequalities had generally been none too successful. The courts have applied the doctrine of "substantial equality" rather than that of identical opportunities and facilities. The result has been that the disparity has tended to increase rather than diminish since 1920.[23] It has been recently held that the doctrine of "substantial equality" permits some inequalities; thus, the Court of Appeals of Maryland, in applying the doctrine of "substantial equality" in 1937, ruled that the "allowance of separate treatment at all involves allowance of some incidental differences and some inequalities in meeting practical problems presented."[24] In the thinking of Negroes,

---

19 Mangum, *op. cit.*, 128 f.

20 N.A.A.C.P., *Teachers' Salaries in Black and White* (New York, 1942), 3; United States Office of Education, *Statistics of State School Systems, 1937–1938* (Washington, D. C., 1939), 134.

21 Wilkerson, *op. cit.*, 8 f.

22 T. J. Woofter, *Negro Problems in Cities* (New York, 1928), 207.

23 Horace M. Bond, *The Education of the Negro in the American Social Order* (New York, 1934), 225–32; Charles H. Thompson, "Court Action the Only Reasonable Remedy to Remove Immediate Abuses in the Negro Separate School," *Journal of Negro History,* IV (1935), 419. The cost held necessary in order to establish educational equality as between Negroes and whites in the South has been variously estimated at from an additional $400,000 a year to a total of $56,000,000. See Wilkerson, *op. cit.*, 58; New York *Times,* April 27, 1941, IV, 9. However, Lou Ethel Martin, "The Effect of Court Decisions on Negro Education in the South," unpublished master's thesis, Howard University, 1933, 10, concludes that court action has resulted in better educational facilities for Negroes in the South.

24 *Williams v. Zimmerman,* 192 Atl. 355.

the manner in which the doctrine of "substantial equality" was applied by the courts up to 1936, in regard to matters of education, permitted the concealment of violations of the Fourteenth Amendment.

Prior to 1936 court action invoking the Fourteenth Amendment in questions of educational opportunities for Negroes was confined almost exclusively to various aspects of the primary and secondary educational levels. Little or no emphasis was placed upon provisions for collegiate, graduate, and professional educational opportunities for Negroes. However, developments in Negro life during the twenties and early thirties demanded that Negroes have access to such opportunities. Increased standards and requirements in teaching and in professional and economic life made training on the graduate and professional level essential. Moreover, by 1930 Negro students were graduating from American colleges in sufficient numbers to call attention to the general absence of such facilities in southern states.[25] As late as 1937, graduate instruction was available to Negro students in only three publicly supported Negro institutions in the South, and professional training was available in none. Nine southern states made no provisions whatsoever for graduate or professional training for Negroes despite the fact that such was provided at public expense for white students.[26]

Late in 1935 the National Association for the Advancement of Colored People launched an aggressive campaign against racial discrimination and inequality in public education. The campaign quickly won the active support of Negroes throughout the country. Organized effort, which had brought legal victories in the *Lee* and *Scottsboro* cases, seemed to have resulted in new evidences of racial solidarity. The movement opened with almost simultaneous action being initiated in five southern states for the admission of Negro students to the universities maintained by

---

[25] Charles S. Johnson, *The Negro College Graduate* (Chapel Hill, N. C., 1938), 10.

[26] United States Office of Education, *National Survey of Higher Education for Negroes* (Washington, D. C., 1944), I, 42; Wilkerson, *op. cit.*, 63–66.

the state.[27] It should be noted that the defense of "substantial equality" could not be easily relied on by the states in question; none of them had made any provisions for graduate or professional education for Negroes within the state. Appraising the movement, one Negro newspaper stated:

> . . . theoretically it looks like a movement to get Negro pupils admitted to state universities. Legally the action takes that form. But realistically, it is a movement to procure for colored people educational needs which they are now denied, and to remove a discrimination which denies them the same privileges under law that other citizens enjoy.[28]

Legal action under the Fourteenth Amendment between 1936 and 1943 was largely concerned with gaining the admission of Negro students to state universities in states which excluded them from such opportunities.

Prior to 1936 some southern states had enacted out-state scholarship laws, an ingenious device for providing "equal but separate" university opportunities for Negroes. Such legislation usually provided for the payment of tuition for Negro students, who attended universities outside the state, for courses offered to white students at the state university from which Negroes were excluded by law. Out-state scholarships were enacted by Missouri in 1921 and 1929 and by Maryland in 1933.[29] By 1938 out-state scholarship laws had been enacted by eight southern and border states. In most instances such laws were considered most inadequate, for the money appropriated was sufficient to provide only a very limited number of scholarships for the large number of prospective applicants.[30]

---

27 Charles H. Houston, "Educational Inequalities Must Go," *Crisis*, XLII (1935), 300 f.

28 Norfolk *Journal and Guide*, August 31, 1935, 8.

29 *Missouri Statutes Annotated* (St. Paul, 1932), LVII, 7328; Washington *Afro-American*, July 8, 1933, 1. The President of the University of Maryland was reported to have advised that no publicity be given the Maryland law because "it would bring a flood of applicants."

30 North Carolina, Committee to Study Public Schools and Colleges for Colored People, *Report and Recommendations* (Raleigh, N. C., 1938), 60;

Probably the first suit seeking to compel the admission of a Negro student to a southern state university was that brought in Durham, North Carolina, in April, 1932. Here the effort was made to compel the admission of Thomas Holcutt to the School of Pharmacy of the University of North Carolina by writ of mandamus. The court ruled that mandamus was not the proper remedy for Holcutt's allegation of educational discrimination and dismissed the suit. Holcutt proved a bad choice for a test case due to his lack of the necessary qualifications for admission; therefore, no attempt was made to appeal the judgment.[31]

Despite expressions of the southern press that such action was ill-advised and that those making the effort were either "reds" or "lunatics," the movement against the exclusion of Negroes from state universities continued with a test case before the courts of Maryland. In May, 1935, Donald Murray, a Negro resident of Baltimore who met all of the requirements for admission, sued for a writ of mandamus to compel the authorities of the University of Maryland to admit him. He contended that his exclusion, solely because of race and color, was a violation of the Fourteenth Amendment.[32] Commenting on the suit, the Baltimore *Evening Sun* of May 6, 1935 stated: "The Negro who has brought suit to force his way into the law school of the University of Maryland may cost the State a lot of money before the thing is over."[33] The court granted the writ ordering Murray's admission as a law student to the University. Officials of the University appealed the judgment.

Wilkerson, *op. cit.,* 61; C. S. Holloway, "The Fourteenth Amendment and Negro Education," 51, unpublished master's thesis, directed by Professor Richard J. Purcell, Catholic University of America, 1942. None of the states making such provisions were those with the heaviest concentration of Negro population. No state, with twenty to thirty per cent of its population Negro, provided scholarships for graduate and professional study. See Wilkerson, *op. cit.,* 61.

[31] New York *Times,* April 2, 1933, IV, 7; 45 *Yale Law Journal,* 1298; *Negro Year-Book,* 1937–1938, 140.

[32] *University of Maryland v. Murray,* 169 Md. 478 (1936). The case was financed by the National Association for the Advancement of Colored People and argued by the Association's attorneys.

[33] Quoted in Norfolk *Journal and Guide,* May 11, 1935, 8.

Counsel for the University advanced two contentions: (1) that the law school by reason of its character and organization was not a state agency and, therefore, not bound by the limitations of the Fourteenth Amendment and (2) that the Maryland out-state scholarship act established substantially equal educational opportunities for Negroes.[34] There was no question but that the law school was an agency of the state government, decided the court. No matter what its origin, character, or organization, the fact that the state of Maryland provided legal education for its citizens in the law school was sufficient to establish it as a state agency. Furthermore, as a state agency, it was subject to the constitutional limitations which might be applied to state action.[35] The court proceeded to define equality of treatment, declaring that:

> The requirement of equal treatment would seem to be clearly enough one of equal treatment in respect to any one facility or opportunity furnished to citizens rather than a balance in state bounty to be struck from the expenditures and provisions for each race generally. . . . Expenditures of the State for the education of the latter [Negro] in schools and colleges have been extensive; but however they may compare with the provisions for whites, they would not justify the exclusion of colored citizens from the enjoyment of any one facility furnished by the State.[36]

It was pointed out, however, that equality of privilege did not mean that the privilege must be provided both races in the same place. The choice of the method employed in maintaining equality—in the same or in different places—was a matter of state discretion. Thus, the court reaffirmed the constitutionality of educational segregation.

The court would not agree with the contention that out-state scholarships, like those made available to Negro students by the Maryland act, maintained equality of educational opportunity. The amount of money appropriated for the purpose and the num-

---

[34] 169 Md. 482, 484, 487.

[35] *Ibid.*, 482.

[36] *Ibid.*, 484.

ber of applicants for the limited number of scholarships made it uncertain that any one of the applicants would receive any one of the scholarships offered.[37] Furthermore, the necessity of going outside the state for legal training involved additional expense and the deprivation of an opportunity to study the law and procedure of one's own state. It was impossible, thought the court, that the "rather slender chance for any one applicant at an opportunity to attend an outside law school, at increased expense," could fulfill the mandate of substantially equal educational opportunities for both races. The court concluded that, since no Negro law school had been decided upon and "only an inadequate substitute" provided, the Negro student must be admitted to the one state university where legal education was provided by the state.[38]

Much significance was attached to the decision in the *Murray* case because it was the first decision of its kind. An analysis of the decision reveals three important facts. First, while the doctrine of "substantial equality" was maintained, it was more narrowly defined than had been the practice. As it applied to educational opportunities, it was defined as a specific rather than as a general doctrine; it was appraised in terms of specific educational opportunities, not the state's general educational program. Secondly, the decision suggests a more realistic approach on the part of a state court in appraising the state's provisions for Negro education than had been the custom. Finally, an out-state

[37] *Ibid.*, 486. Between June 1, 1935, and June 18, 1935, one hundred and thirteen Negro students applied for fifty available scholarships. An investigation by the National Association for the Advancement of Colored People revealed that one hundred and eighty-seven applicants were left unprovided for under the scholarship law of 1935. N.A.A.C.P., "Press Release," February 7, 1936, cited in 45 *Yale Law Journal*, 1299.

[38] Donald Murray was admitted to the School of Law of the University of Maryland and was graduated in June, 1938. A second Negro student, Calvin Douglass, was graduated in 1940. See Washington *Afro-American*, June 11, 1938, 1; Holloway, *loc. cit.*, 50–51. It was reported that when the Maryland legislature enacted a new scholarship law in 1937, which appropriated increased funds, President Harry C. Byrd of the University of Maryland sought a ruling as to the authority to oust Murray. The act in question was found not to be retroactive, and the idea was dropped. Washington *Afro-American*, July 3, 1937, 9; also issue of October 2, 1937, 4.

scholarship law, upon which southern states heavily relied to substantiate their claims of providing equal educational opportunities for both races, had been held insufficient to fulfill the mandate of equal protection of the law.

One of the immediate effects of the decision in the *Murray* case was an intensification of the campaign to secure graduate and professional educational opportunities for Negroes in separate-school states.. Almost immediately there was an increase in the number of Negro applicants for admission to the Universities of Maryland, Virginia, and Missouri.[39] Plans were made for initiating legal action in several southern states similar to that which had proved successful in Maryland. Some southern states, Kentucky and West Virginia among them, met the challenge by the enactment of out-state scholarship laws and by increased appropriations for Negro institutions within their states.[40]

While the decision in the *Murray* case was considered a significant legal victory, those directing the movement realized the necessity of a ruling by the United States Supreme Court on the question of the sufficiency of out-state scholarships to fulfill the demand of equal protection of law. Nothing short of such a ruling could make the Maryland position binding upon the states. A case arising in Missouri presented an opportunity to bring the question before the Supreme Court. Lloyd Gaines, a Negro student, applied for and was refused admission to the law school of the University of Missouri. He filed suit for a writ of mandamus claiming the refusal of admission violated his rights under the Fourteenth Amendment. The state Circuit Court dismissed the suit and this judgment was affirmed by the Supreme Court of Missouri.[41] The latter court held that the separation of races for purposes of education was constitutional and that

[39] Charles H. Houston, "Cracking Closed University Doors," in Fitzhugh L. Styles, *Negroes and the Law,* 90. Virginius Dabney, editor of the Richmond *Times-Dispatch,* declared that Negroes were aiming at greater state support of Negro schools rather than the admission of Negro students to state universities in southern states. New York *Times,* April 2, 1933, IV, 7.

[40] Henry J. McGuinn, "Equality of Educational Opportunity," *Journal of Negro Education,* VIII (1939), 162 f.

[41] *State* ex rel. *Gaines v. Canada,* 113 S. W. (2d) 783 (1938).

the opportunity offered by the state for a legal education in an adjacent state was substantially equal to the provision made for legal education for white students at the University of Missouri.[42] Gaines appealed to the United States Supreme Court which granted writ of certiorari to review the case.

Counsel for Canada, the registrar of the University of Missouri, contended that no federal question was involved in the case and, therefore, the Supreme Court lacked jurisdiction. The courts of Missouri, he argued, had recognized the petitioner's constitutional right to an equal opportunity for a legal education and ruled that the state afforded such. Gaines had failed to avail himself of the opportunity for a legal education which the state afforded. Furthermore, the state had already declared its intention of establishing a law school at Lincoln University, the state university for Negroes; pending such action and as a temporary matter, provisions made for the payment of tuition for Negro students, who had to go outside of the state for a legal education, should be upheld.[43]

The majority opinion was written by Chief Justice Hughes and read on December 12, 1938. He was convinced that the allegation of an educational discrimination was sufficient to establish the Court's jurisdiction in the case. The provisions made by Missouri for the legal education of Negroes were held insufficient to satisfy the essential demands of equality of educational opportunity, even though they might be considered mere temporary expedients. Missouri's declared intent to establish a law school at Lincoln University "whenever necessary and practical" was a commendable act, declared the Chief Justice, "but the fact remains that instruction in law for Negroes is not now afforded by the State, either at Lincoln University or elsewhere within the State."[44] Moreover, Negroes were excluded from the law school which the state had established for white students. The Court concluded: "This discrimination, unrelieved, would constitute a denial of equal protection."[45]

---

[42] *Ibid.*, 790.

[43] *Missouri* ex rel. *Gaines v. Canada,* 305 U. S. 339, 340.

[44] *Ibid.*, 345.

[45] *Ibid.*

Despite the state's declaration of intent to establish a law school for Negroes, the Court found the purposes still unfulfilled. Moreover, the determination of "necessity" and "practicability" had been left to the discretion of the curators of Lincoln University. Thus, it was held that there was no mandatory duty placed upon anyone to make legal education available to the petitioner within the state.

Chief Justice Hughes then turned to a consideration of the question of the sufficiency of an out-state scholarship to satisfy the requirements of equal protection. He defined the scope of the question as follows: "The basic consideration is not what opportunities other states provide or how good they are, but as to what opportunities Missouri itself furnishes to white students and denies to negroes solely upon the ground of color."[46] Missouri's act of establishing a special privilege for whites which was denied Negroes, solely on account of color, was held to be a discrimination which worked a denial of equal protection of law. Out-state scholarships did not remove the discrimination, said the Chief Justice, for "the obligation of the state to give the protection of equal laws can be performed only where its laws operate, that is, within its own jurisdiction. It is there that the equality of legal right must be maintained."[47] In the absence of provisions for legal education for Negroes within the state, the Court ruled that the petitioner was entitled to be admitted to the law school of the University of Missouri.

The opinion in this case was a divided one with Justices McReynolds and Butler dissenting from the opinion of the Court. They felt that Missouri had made a conscientious effort to extend equal educational opportunities to the petitioner; it had attempted to solve a difficult problem in good faith. Though the provision

---

[46] *Ibid.*, 348. This position closely followed that taken by the Supreme Court of California in *Piper v. Big Pine School District of Inyo County*, 226 Pac. 926 (Calif., 1924). Here the court ruled that education was a function of the state which could not be shifted to the Federal Government and that the expense involved in establishing a separate school for Indians could not justify the failure of the state to provide equal educational facilities for them. In the absence of such facilities, Indian students were entitled to attend the schools established for white students.

[47] *Missouri* ex rel. *Gaines v. Canada,* 305 U. S. 350.

made for legal education for Negroes was outside of the state, it offered an adequate opportunity for study. Cautioning the majority as to the effects of its decision, Justice McReynolds said: "The State should not be unduly hampered through theorization inadequately restrained by experience." [48]

Reactions to the decision in the *Gaines* case were as partisan as the issue involved. The Negro press considered it "the most significant victory for Negro rights in the highest court of the land in the past decade" and compared it with the decision which outlawed the "grandfather clause." [49] Some held that the decision would not only make all types of graduate and professional education available to Negroes in southern states, where it had been denied,[50] but it would affect all phases of Negro education.[51] Moreover, it would serve to re-open the whole question of the constitutionality of educational classifications based on race and result in a closer examination of the doctrine of "substantial equality" by the courts.[52] The most significant result of the decision was held to be the invalidation of out-state scholarships as a means of fulfilling the state's obligation of providing equal educational opportunities for both races. This was viewed as a most encouraging extension of the guarantees of the Fourteenth Amendment in regard to Negro rights.

More cautious appraisal of the effects of the decision in the *Gaines* case held that, while the position of the Court was both constitutionally and socially sound, the far-reaching results expected from the decision would perhaps not materialize.[53] There was some doubt that the educational facilities, provided for

---

[48] *Ibid.*, 354.

[49] Norfolk *Journal and Guide*, December 24, 1938, 9; "University of Missouri Case Won," *Crisis*, XLVI (1939), 10.

[50] New York *Times*, December 13, 1938, 1.

[51] Willis D. Curtis, "Comments on the Gaines Decision," 24 *Cornell Law Quarterly*, 422; Elsa Kievets, "Comments on Negro Educational Facilities," 13 *Southern California Law Review*, 75.

[52] Kievets, *loc. cit.*, 75. One opinion held that, after the *Gaines* decision, there was little possibility that the Supreme Court would "further whittle away" the doctrine of "substantial equality" as it applied to education. See 6 *University of Chicago Law Review*, 338.

[53] Curtis, *loc. cit.*, 421.

Negroes under the mandate of the *Gaines* decision, would be either the equal of those provided for white students or as advantageous as the opportunities offered under out-state scholarships.

Unfavorable criticism of the decision was based upon considerations of impracticability and the financial burden which would result from its application. It was based upon the conception of some " mystical impregnability of state borders," said one commentator, for " if the opportunity for an education outside the state is made available, why is its [the state's] duty not performed? " [54] Despite the decision or its effects, southern states were determined to maintain their traditional policy of separate schools. It was admitted, however, that the maintenance of separate schools at the graduate and professional level would impose " a severe and disproportionate burden " upon some states.[55]

Missouri, the state most immediately affected, made plans for complying with the decision. A statute was enacted which provided for the reorganization of Lincoln University and the establishment of a law school there by September 1, 1939. The legislature appropriated $200,000 for that purpose.[56] There was considerable opposition on the part of Negroes to this proposal. It was looked upon as an attempt to evade the Supreme Court's ruling which would set the example for other states, similarly situated, to follow. Should the solution which Missouri was adopting be allowed to stand, southern states would set up weak graduate schools for Negroes, to satisfy the law, which would be in no manner substantially equal to those provided for white students.[57] Efforts to prevent the establishment of the proposed

---

54 8 *Fordham Law Review,* 263. See also John B. Breckenridge, " Racial Segregation for Purposes of Education," 27 *Kentucky Law Review,* 238.

55 Richmond *Times-Dispatch,* December 15, 1938, 10. For a discussion of proposed means of evading the decision, see Frank T. Miller, " Comments on the Admission of Negroes to State Universities," 17 *North Carolina Law Review,* 285.

56 Missouri, *Revised Statutes,* 1939, 283; St. Louis *Daily Globe-Democrat,* December 14, 1938, B, 2.

57 Glenn Hutchinson, " Jim Crow Challenged in Southern Universities," *Crisis,* XLVI (1939), 103; Lucille Bluford, " Missouri ' Shows ' the Supreme

law school at Lincoln University were unsuccessful.[58]

Dissatisfaction over the manner in which Missouri had complied with the Supreme Court's ruling in the *Gaines* case called forth a second attack against the denial of admission of Negro students to the University of Missouri. Within a month of the *Gaines* decision, a second suit was filed in the case of *Bluford v. Canada.*[59] The case arose out of the application of Thelma Bluford, a Negro citizen of Missouri, for admission to the Graduate School of Journalism of the University of Missouri and the denial of admission.[60] It was claimed that the refusal of permission to register was a violation of the "equal protection"

Court," *Crisis,* XLVI (1939), 231-232; Narvel P. Barksdale, "The Gaines Case and Its Effects on Negro Education in Missouri," *School and Society,* LI (1940), 311; Holloway, *loc. cit.,* 55–58.

58 Washington *Afro-American,* August 12, 1939, 1–2. The law school was opened on September 21, 1939, with thirty students enrolled. The enrollment steadily decreased until there were no students enrolled and no new applicants for admission in February, 1944. This, plus the fact that the funds set aside for its maintenance were exhausted, resulted in the closing of the law school on February 1, 1944. An editorial in the Chicago *Defender,* January 29, 1944, 12, criticizing the Lincoln University venture, stated: "The narrow thinking of the curators and legislators resulted in an unjustifiable waste of the taxpayers' money." Prior to the closing of the law school, there was evidence that some Missouri legislators and officials were becoming convinced that the burden of maintaining a separate law school for Negroes was both excessive and unwise. One official stated: "We'd just as well tell the Negroes to go ahead and register at Columbia [University of Missouri] and if the students don't object, let them stay there." Quoted in *Crisis,* XLVIII (1941), 292. See also Editorial, Chicago *Defender,* January 29, 1944, 12; Pittsburgh *Courier,* January 29, 1944, 5. Since the closing of the law school at Lincoln University, it appears that no legal action has been taken to force the admission of Negro students to the law school of the tax-supported University of Missouri. Such action would appear to succeed in the absence of similar facilities for Negro students.

59 32 Fed. Supp. 707 (D.C.W.D. Mo., 1940).

60 Norfolk *Journal and Guide,* February 11, 1939. The applicant was told: "The decision of the Supreme Court in the Gaines case has not yet become final, but is still pending in the Supreme Court of Missouri for further consideration. The long established policy of the State cannot be altered pending final judgment in the Gaines case." Washington *Afro-American,* February 11, 1939, 1.

clause of the Fourteenth Amendment. It was further contended that, in keeping with the Supreme Court ruling in *Missouri* ex rel. *Gaines v. Canada,* if the desired instruction was available to white students at the University of Missouri and not immediately available to Negroes at Lincoln University, the plaintiff was entitled to admission.

In determining whether or not the plaintiff was entitled to admission to the University of Missouri, the United States District Court pointed out that " the imminent and mandatory establishment of the facilities [desired] would temporarily excuse discrimination." Only in the face of an " impelling necessity to secure to the citizen his constitutional rights " would the court be justified in changing the state's long-established policy of the separation of races.[61] Bluford had no cause for action, the United States District Court decided, in that she had failed to give the authorities ample time to furnish the type of instruction desired but not currently offered at Lincoln University. Unless this was done, " Lincoln University would have to maintain at all times all departments of instruction, whether used or not, which are available at the University of Missouri." [62] The court concluded that the state had disregarded none of the plaintiff's rights " in not maintaining in non-use facilities which no one had requested or indicated a desire to use." [63] Therefore, the suit to compel admission to the University of Missouri was dismissed.

The campaign for the admission of Negro students to state

[61] 32 Fed. Supp. 711.

[62] *Ibid.* A school of journalism was opened at Lincoln University on February 5, 1942. However, it closed on the same day that the law school closed because of its small enrollment. Norfolk *Journal and Guide,* January 24, 1944, 2; Holloway, *loc. cit.,* 59; Chicago *Defender,* February 12, 1944, 2.

[63] Following up the two Missouri cases, application was made by Negro students to the state universities in North Carolina, South Carolina, Georgia, Texas, and Tennessee. However, all of the cases which resulted were indecisive. Except for the admission of two Negro students to the School of Law of the University of Maryland, it appears that no Negro students were admitted to any of the state institutions in any southern state. See *Crisis,* XLVI (1939), 341; Holloway, *loc. cit.,* 12.

universities in the southern and border states reached its climax in the two cases directed against the University of Missouri. One unquestionable result of this litigation was an increase in opportunities for graduate instruction for Negro students in southern states. In the face of the Supreme Court's ruling that equal educational opportunities must be afforded within the state, southern states were compelled to consider the problem of graduate instruction for Negro students. Pledged to the maintenance of separate schools, there appeared but one line of action to follow—to take the necessary measures to provide graduate instruction for Negro students which was "substantially equal" to that provided for and enjoyed by white students. North Carolina began studying the problem while the *Gaines* case was under litigation. A commission appointed to consider the needs of Negro education in the state recommended that "some satisfactory plan for providing graduate and professional education in the state shall be determined by the Legislature of 1939" and that substantial funds be appropriated for that purpose.[64] This recommendation resulted in the establishment of a graduate school and a law school at one of the existing state supported Negro colleges on September 25, 1939.[65]

Maryland took a similar step in 1939. When the *Gaines* case declared the insufficiency of out-state scholarships to satisfy the demand of equal protection of law under the Fourteenth Amendment, Maryland began considering plans to provide graduate instruction for Negroes within the state. The Commission on Scholarships for Negroes recommended the purchase and incorporation of Morgan College, a privately owned Negro college, into the state system and the development of graduate instruction there for Negro students. The purchase was completed in June,

---

[64] North Carolina Commission to Study Public Schools and Colleges for Colored People, *Report and Recommendations,* 10, 57–61.

[65] In contrast to the sentiment in Missouri against accepting anything less than the admission of Negro students to the state university, Negro leaders and educators in North Carolina supported the plan for developing graduate work at one of the existing Negro schools. See Norfolk *Journal and Guide,* April 18, 1942, 20.

1939.[66] Virginia also established a graduate school at its state college for Negroes and Georgia began considering the problem in 1943.[67]

It may be safely asserted that none of the graduate schools for Negroes, established in compliance with the ruling in the *Gaines* case, were on a par with those maintained for whites.[68] Both the provisions and appropriations made for the purpose were grossly inadequate; and in all probability, the question of substantial equality in regard to these provisions will be carried before the courts. Nevertheless, such provisions as were made constituted a first-step in the direction of greater equality of educational opportunity for Negroes as this concept applies to higher education.

The duplication of professional schools, except for law schools and schools of journalism, has not been attempted by southern states; and to the present time, there has been practically no litigation in regard to other types of professional education. To a great extent, the cost of maintaining two identical state professional schools in each field would be almost prohibitive in poor states. The Southern University Conference, in November, 1939, proposed the establishment of regional universities for Negroes, supported by all of the states of the region as a means of meeting the problem. While this proposal has gained wide acceptance among southern educators and state officials,[69] there

---

66 Maryland Commission on Scholarships for Negroes, *Report* (Baltimore, 1939), 3–8; Washington *Afro-American,* June 10, 1939, 4.

67 Pittsburgh *Courier,* May 1, 1943, 1.

68 Mangum, *op. cit.,* 106 f. Dr. James E. Shepherd, President of North Carolina College for Negroes, expressed the conviction that graduate courses at that institution were substantially the same instruction given white students at the University of North Carolina. It should be noted that twenty of the twenty-three teachers in the graduate school at this institution in 1941 were regular professors from the University of North Carolina and Duke University who taught courses at the Negro institution on a part time basis. Washington *Afro-American,* August 9, 1941, 25.

69 New York *Times,* November 12, 1939, IV, 10; Washington *Afro-American,* January 21, 1940, 4; Pittsburgh *Courier,* May 15, 1943, 6. In view of the Supreme Court's mandate that equal protection of law must be provided within the state, it is probable that such action would be held unconstitutional if presented to the Court for a ruling.

are some who hold that state revenues should be supplemented by federal aid.[70]

While the campaign to increase educational opportunities for Negroes in southern states was in progress, the Fourteenth Amendment was invoked against another aspect of educational inequality as practiced in southern states. Southern states have traditionally paid Negro public school teachers lower salaries than were paid to white teachers of the same classification, level, and experience. The emphasis on equal educational opportunities for Negroes, during the period 1936–1943, caused this type of salary discrimination to be singled out for attack; such discrimination appeared to violate the constitutional guarantee of equal protection of law.

The extent of salary discrimination against Negro public school teachers was made known through a series of studies conducted between 1936 and 1940. In North Carolina, white public school teachers holding class A certificates were paid $990 per year in 1938 while Negro teachers holding the same certificate were paid $770. A committee studying the problem recommended that "a reduction in the salary differential would be very wise in 1939." [71] Salary schedules in Maryland in 1939 ranged from $600 to $1750 for white elementary teachers and from $360 to $1170 for Negro elementary teachers.[72] Similar differentials were found in other southern states. It was estimated that Negro teachers in seventeen states maintaining separate schools received from fifty to sixty-one cents to every dollar received by white teachers for salaries.[73] The greatest disparities were observed in states with the greatest concentration of Negro population. The National Association for the Advancement of Colored People claimed that more than $25,000,000 were lost to Negro public school teachers annually because they were Negroes, this figure representing the

[70] United States Office of Education, *National Survey of Higher Education for Negroes,* I, xi, 103.

[71] North Carolina Commission to Study Schools and Colleges for Colored People, *op. cit.,* 9, 31; also Bond, *op. cit.,* 155 f.

[72] *Maryland Code Annotated* (Baltimore, 1939), 2924, 2967; *Mills v. Bd. of Ed. of Anne Arundel Co.,* 30 Fed. Supp. 247 (1939).

[73] N.A.A.C.P., *Teachers' Salaries in Black and White,* 4; Doxey Wilkerson, *Special Problems of Negro Education,* 24–28.

discrepancy between salaries paid to Negro and to white public school teachers in fifteen separate school states.[74] Commenting on salary differentials based on race, a foreign educator remarked:

> The black teacher ought perhaps to be paid even better than the white one. First of all, their number is smaller in proportion, which gives them more work. Again, they are out to be a model and living example to the population and qualified guides to show them the beauties and advantages of civilization. Education must create needs among the Negroes.[75]

The motives and attitudes supporting salary differentials as between Negro and white public school teachers in the South are varied indeed. But in the main they are part of the southern attitude which holds that Negroes should not be paid equal salaries for equal work. In many instances where salary differentials have been frankly admitted, the following reasons have been given for the discrimination: (1) the cost of living of white teachers and principals was higher than that of Negro teachers and principals; (2) it was necessary to pay white teachers more to enable them "to maintain their standing as respectable citizens of the community"; (3) Negro teachers are more easily hired than white teachers; and (4) white teachers possess greater teaching qualifications than Negro teachers.[76] The question of salary discrimination can be easily recognized as part of the larger problem of unequal educational opportunities for Negroes in the South.

A movement to compel the equalization of teachers' salaries was begun in 1938 under the leadership of the National Association for the Advancement of Colored People. The Association

---

[74] N.A.A.C.P., *Teachers' Salaries in Black and White,* 4. In 1941 the Secretary of the Georgia Education Association estimated that $75,000,000 would be required to equalize teachers' salaries in the South. See New York *Times,* April 27, 1941, IV, 9.

[75] Robert Rothschild, "A Belgian's View of Negro Schools," *Journal of Negro Education,* IV (1935), 181–82.

[76] *Thomas v. Hibbetts,* 46 Fed. Supp. 370 (D.C. Tenn., 1942); Leonard E. Meece, *Negro Education in Kentucky* in University of Kentucky Bureau of School Service, *Bulletin* (Lexington, Kentucky, 1938), No. 3, 103, 117.

held that salary equalization was a necessary step in the progress of Negroes toward cultural and economic equality in the United States in that it would help to open the door of American citizenship even wider for Negroes. Five suits for equal salaries were filed by Negro public school teachers in five southern states in 1938, which included Maryland, Virginia, and North Carolina.[77] These suits were constitutionally supported by the " equal protection " clause of the Fourteenth Amendment. It was held that the constitutional guarantees of equal protection of law prohibited the state and its agencies from discriminating against Negro teachers in regard to salary, solely on account of race and color.

The first legal victory in the campaign for salary equalization was that in the case of *Mills v. Board of Education of Anne Arundel County* in 1939.[78] However, in an earlier case, Walter Mills, a Negro elementary school principal, brought suit to compel the equalization of his salary with that paid white elementary school principals of similar classification. The suit was dismissed because it was brought against the wrong parties; the mistake had been made of naming general state officers rather than county officers.[79] Prior to this action, the Maryland Democratic State Convention pledged the equalization of salaries " at the earliest possible time." [80] Nothing was done to redeem this pledge until legal action was initiated. At that time a proposal was made by county officials to increase the salaries of Negro teachers in Anne Arundel County ten per cent in 1939 and ten per cent each succeeding year " until they approximate the state minimum for white teachers." [81] Under this proposal, it was estimated that salary equalization would be attained in four to five years, and it was conditioned upon the discontinuance of legal action. The plan was unacceptable to Negro teachers and a second suit was filed by Walter Mills.

Counsel for Mills contended before the court that despite

[77] Norfolk *Journal and Guide,* January 8, 1938, 1; February 5, 1938, 20; April 30, 1938, 1.

[78] 30 Fed. Supp. 245.

[79] *Mills v. Lowndes,* 26 Fed. Supp. 792, 803.

[80] Norfolk *Journal and Guide,* October 8, 1938, 1.

[81] 30 Fed. Supp. 250.

uniform requirements, Negro teachers in the county were paid less than white teachers, solely because of race and color. This, it was urged, constituted an unconstitutional discrimination under the Fourteenth Amendment. The Board of Education of Anne Arundel County admitted that a very "substantial difference" existed between the salaries paid Negro and white teachers. However, the statutory discrimination did not apply to Negro teachers as such, but to "all teachers in colored schools whether white or colored." The discrimination, therefore, was not against Negro teachers, but against the colored school.[82] Moreover, the practice of unequal salaries seemed sound in that it had always existed. The court had to determine whether the statute which provided for salary differentials between Negro and white teachers resulted in an unconstitutional discrimination which was prohibited by the Fourteenth Amendment.

In deciding the case, the court pointed to the unusual fact that, comparing the salaries of two hundred and forty-three white and ninety-one Negro teachers, no one Negro teacher received as much salary as any one white teacher. No evidence had been produced to satisfy the claim that white teachers were more efficient than Negro teachers. Moreover, "efficiency and superior professional attainments explain greater compensation to individuals for particular positions but cannot account for the difference between $1075 [the salary paid Mills] and $1550 which by the County scale would have to be paid to any white principal of a comparable school."[83] Thus, the discrimination could not have been based upon the test of efficiency.

The evidence led the court to the conclusion that an unconstitutional discrimination was practiced in the County. Declared the court: "The plaintiff, as a colored teacher, is unconstitutionally discriminated against in the practice of his profession by the discrimination made between white and colored teachers by the County School Board of Anne Arundel County."[84] The plaintiff was entitled to an injunction against the continuation of the practice. The County argued that salary equalization would

[82] *Ibid.*, 247.
[83] *Ibid.*, 248.
[84] *Ibid.*, 249.

impose an inordinate financial burden and result in an increase in the tax-rate. But such a contention could not justify a disregard of an individual's constitutional rights. "I am not unmindful of the difficult financial position which is thus created for the County," concluded the opinion, "but these considerations cannot control the supreme law of the land as expressed in the Fourteenth Amendment and the implementing acts of Congress." [85]

Success in the Maryland salary discrimination suit stimulated similar legal action in other southern areas. While the Maryland case, which was argued by the legal staff of the National Association for the Advancement of Colored People, presented both a precedent and a technique for initiating action against other southern jurisdictions, two difficulties had to be overcome. In the deep-South, where salary differentials were greatest, Negro leadership dared not be aggressive and there was a great deal of hesitancy in initiating legal action for the equalization of salaries. Furthermore, school boards frequently refused to re-elect persons who had previously brought actions relative to salary and position.[86]

The campaign for salary equalization in Virginia was carried on simultaneously with that in Maryland. The first suit filed by a Negro public school teacher, that against the Norfolk School Board, was dropped when the teacher was dismissed.[87] A second suit was brought by Melvin O. Alston and the Norfolk Teachers Association, an organization of Negro public school teachers, against the Norfolk School Board. The suit asked for a declara-

---

[85] *Ibid.*, 250. The Baltimore *Sun*, November 24, 1939, 10, observed that while the decision raised certain financial difficulties, it was a just ruling and in line with the recent steps taken by the state (the purchase of Morgan College) for the improvement of Negro education in Maryland.

[86] N.A.A.C.P., *Teachers' Salaries in Black and White*, 10; *Crisis*, L (1943), 180 f. Well illustrating this point is the advice given to a conference of Negro principals in Mississippi in 1943 by the State Superintendent of Education. He advised that court action for salary equalization "would result in the loss of friendship of those with sympathetic interest in Negro educational progress in Mississippi." Norfolk *Journal and Guide*, October 23, 1943, 3.

[87] Norfolk *Journal and Guide*, November 5, 1938, 20; also issue of June 14, 1939, 2.

tory judgment to the effect that the practice of paying Negro teachers, of the same qualifications and experience, at a lower rate than white teachers was a violation of due process and equal protection under the Fourteenth Amendment.[88] The United States District Court dismissed the suit on the grounds that it had included the Norfolk Teachers Association, which was held to be an unnecessary party, and that Alston had waived his constitutional right by entering into a contract to teach for a year at the salary stated in the contract. Alston appealed this judgment to the United States Circuit Court of Appeals for the Fourth Circuit.[89]

Three issues had to be determined by the Circuit Court: (1) whether an unconstitutional discrimination was practiced in fixing school teachers' salaries; (2) whether the plaintiffs' rights were infringed by such discrimination; and (3) whether plaintiffs had waived the right to complain of discrimination by entering into contract with the School Board for the current year. Judge Parker answered affirmatively in regard to the first two issues and negatively in regard to the last. An examination of the salary schedule for 1939, which established a minimum salary of $784 for male Negro high school teachers and a minimum of $1200 for male white high school teachers of the same classification, led to the conclusion that a discriminatory practice resulted. The court declared: "That an unconstitutional discrimination is set forth hardly admits of argument. . . . This is as clear a discrimination on the ground of color as could well be imagined and falls squarely within both the due process and equal protection clauses of the Fourteenth Amendment."[90]

In considering the second and third issues, the court pointed out that certification by the state gave a person a recognized professional status but not the right to teach. However, when a person, certified by the state, applied for a position to teach, he was entitled to have the compensation for that position fixed

---

[88] *Alston et al. v. School Board of City of Norfolk,* 112 Fed. (2d) 992 (1940).

[89] Judge John A. Parker, whose nomination to the Supreme Court bench was successfully opposed by Negroes in 1930, wrote the opinion.

[90] 112 Fed. (2d) 995.

without discrimination because of race. "The plaintiffs, as teachers qualified and subject to employment by the state, are entitled to apply for the positions and to have the discretion of the authorities exercised lawfully and without unconstitutional discrimination as to rate of pay . . . if their applications are accepted," said the court.[91]

Furthermore, by entering into a contract to teach for a specified salary for the current year, the plaintiffs had waived no constitutional right to complain of discrimination. If this was otherwise, reasoned the court, "there would be no practical means of redress for teachers subjected to this unconstitutional discrimination. It is not sound because the State in granting a privilege may not impose conditions which result in the relinquishment of constitutional rights."[92] Moreover, though the contract in question extended only to the current year, the rights under litigation extended beyond that period. On the basis of this reasoning, Alston was entitled to the judgment sought and an injunction restraining the discrimination complained of in fixing salaries after the current year. The case was remanded to the lower court for that purpose.[93] Commenting on the decision, the editor of a newspaper in Richmond, Virginia, stated:

> The existence of such discrimination against Negro teachers as was alleged in the Norfolk case . . . is common knowledge. It is practiced on a wholesale scale with some whites receiving twice as much in some counties for the same duties. It is time this discrimination was ended in the interest of fair play, and also of a better public school system. The Norfolk case may end it, not only in Virginia, but throughout the nation.[94]

Substantial legal victories were won in the Maryland and Virginia salary discrimination cases. Without question they represented a significant extension of the application of the Fourteenth Amendment in regard to Negro rights. But these decisions had

---

[91] *Ibid.*, 997.

[92] *Ibid.*

[93] See Washington *Afro-American,* March 30, 1940, 13, for a discussion of the final settlement of this case.

[94] *Times-Dispatch,* June 21, 1940, 14.

a broader constitutional significance: they applied the Fourteenth Amendment to the state as an employer and established the rule that, in this capacity, the state may not discriminate against those employed, on the basis of race and color.[95] Moreover, these two decisions seem to indicate that whenever state or county school boards establish differential salary schedules for Negro and white public school teachers of the same classification, experience, and performing the same duties, there is *prima facie* evidence of discrimination based on race and color which the state must refute. The position taken by the Federal courts in the salary discrimination cases might also be considered a liberalization of the doctrine of "substantial equality" as it applies to education. Here, however, the emphasis is shifted from the provision of equal educational opportunities to the provision of teachers whose salaries are not fixed in response to racial attitudes and prejudices.

After the *Norfolk* case the movement to equalize salaries gained momentum. Within two years fifty-three city and county school boards in Virginia had made or agreed to make the adjustments necessary to equalize salaries.[96] Legal action was begun in at least five counties in Florida between 1940 and 1942, and terms were agreed upon for equalization.[97] By the end of 1943, similar action had been taken in New Orleans, Louisville, Charleston, South Carolina, and in some counties of North Carolina and Missouri.[98]

An attempt was made in the case of *Thomas v. Hibbetts*,[99] a case arising in Nashville, Tennessee, in 1942, not only to enjoin future salary discrimination, but to recover salary for previous

---

95 53 *Harvard Law Review*, 669; 1 *Bill of Rights Review*, 144.

96 Survey by Walter N. Ridley, Secretary of Virginia State Teachers' Association, Norfolk *Journal and Guide*, August 1, 1942, 6. See also issues of April 18, 1942, 11 and November 15, 1941, 1.

97 *McDaniel v. Bd. of Public Instr. for Escombia County*, 39 Fed. Supp. 638 (D.C.N.D., Fla., 1942); Norfolk *Journal and Guide*, April 18, 1942, 11.

98 "New Orleans Teachers' Suit," *Crisis*, XLIX (1942), 325; Pittsburgh *Courier*, June 24, 1943, 24 and December 4, 1943, 20; Norfolk *Journal and Guide*, July 24, 1943, 10. Maryland equalized salaries in all counties by act of the General Assembly in February, 1941. N.A.A.C.P., *Teachers' Salaries in Black and White*, 6.

99 46 Fed. Supp. 368 (D.C., Tenn.).

service at the equalized rate. The court applied the rule of *Alston v. School Board of City of Norfolk* holding that "the studied and consistent policy" of paying Negro teachers at a lower rate than white teachers was an unconstitutional discrimination. However, the complainant was not entitled to any salary, at the equalized rate, for the period of six years antedating his complaint.

Attempts of southern jurisdictions to evade this application of the Fourteenth Amendment have thus far been relatively unsuccessful. Pleas of financial difficulty have been disallowed by the courts. In some instances, to avoid appearances of obvious salary discrimination based on race, southern jurisdictions have employed rating systems in fixing salaries rather than a fixed salary scale.[100] Such systems as these, granting wide discretionary powers to school authorities in establishing ratings, permit a less obvious discrimination against Negro teachers. However, it is gratifying that few jurisdictions have experimented with such rating systems.

Fair Trials for Negroes

Between 1936 and 1943 efforts by Negroes to secure enforcement of the Fourteenth Amendment seemed to concentrate on the application of its guarantees to problems of Negro education in southern states. However, this was not exclusively the case. Considerable attention was given to the much-litigated issue of the disregard of the constitutional rights of Negro defendants in criminal cases before southern courts. There was a representative number of decisions handed down during this period on the issues of the denial of right of counsel, the exclusion of Negroes from jury service, and mob-dominated trials. A new constitutional issue was under frequent litigation during this period—the issue of whether convictions, based upon confessions secured

---

[100] Under rating systems of this sort, teachers are rated for salary purposes upon such factors as age, character, experience, preparation, teaching ability, general fitness, and general service. The difficulty of accurately measuring such intangibles makes any rating under this system largely an arbitrary one and leaves much opportunity for discrimination against Negroes. See C. D. Hayes, "Notes and Comments," 21 *North Carolina Law Review,* 217–23; Norfolk *Journal and Guide,* October 10, 1942, 2 and December 18, 1943, 2.

through the use of coercive measures, violated due process of law under the Fourteenth Amendment. While there is no evidence that the use of coercion in securing confessions from Negroes accused of crime was more prevalent during the period after 1936 than before, it is significant that ten such cases were decided by the courts between 1936 and 1943. Eight of these were decided by the United States Supreme Court, one by a United States Circuit Court of Appeals, and the other by a state court. All ten of the cases arose in southern jurisdictions with a heavy preponderance of cases from Texas and Alabama.

When the United States Supreme Court handed down its decision in the case of *Brown v. Mississippi*[101] on February 17, 1936, it represented the first decision on the issue of a conviction based upon a confession coerced from a Negro defendant, by a Federal court, during the period 1920–1936. The case arose in Mississippi from the conviction of three Negroes of murder upon the sole evidence of their " free confessions " and their sentence to death. During the trial counsel for the defendants held that the confessions had been secured through violence, in which state officers had participated, and were, therefore, inadmissible as evidence. The request for exclusion of this evidence was refused. On appeal to the Supreme Court of Mississippi, claiming error in the admission of the confessions, that court affirmed the judgment of the lower court.[102] The case was carried to the United States Supreme Court on writ of certiorari.

The decision, written by Chief Justice Hughes and considered both " eloquently condemnatory " and " one of the most vigorous ever pronounced,"[103] reversed the judgment of the Supreme Court of Mississippi. He felt that a deep-rooted principle of justice

---

[101] 297 U. S. 278.

[102] In dissenting from the majority opinion, Justice Griffith of the Supreme Court of Mississippi said: "If mobs and mob methods must be, it would be better that their existence and their methods be kept wholly separate from the courts, that there be no blending of the devices of the mob and the proceedings of the courts . . . by the frills and furbelows of a pretended legal trial." Quoted in the *Daily Clarion-Ledger* (Jackson, Miss.), February 18, 1936, 7.

[103] Washington *Afro-American,* February 22, 1936, 1; *Daily Clarion-Ledger* (Jackson, Miss.), February 18, 1936, 7.

had been violated. In view of the fact that the court had knowledge that the confessions were not voluntary and that state officers had participated in the coercion, such evidence ought not to have been admitted. While the state was free to regulate the procedure of its courts, reasoned the Chief Justice, "the state's freedom in establishing its policy is limited by the requirements of due process of law." [104] The Constitution prohibits "trial by ordeal as a substitute for a jury." He condemned the proceedings of the trial court saying: "It would be difficult to conceive of methods more revolting to the sense of justice than those taken to procure the confessions . . . and the use of the confessions thus obtained was a clear denial of due process." [105]

The state court contended that it should be upheld because counsel for the defendants had failed to move specifically for the exclusion of the confessions.[106] Chief Justice Hughes thought this procedural technicality insufficient to deny the complaint of a violation of due process. He said:

> The complaint is not one of mere error, but of a wrong so fundamental that it makes the whole proceedings a mere pretense of a trial and rendered the conviction and sentence wholly void. . . . The conviction and sentence were void for want of the essential elements of due process and the proceedings thus vitiated could be challenged in any appropriate manner.[107]

The Court concluded that a constitutional right had been denied and, therefore, the judgment of the state court could not stand.[108]

Four years later the question of convictions based on coerced confessions was presented to the Supreme Court in a different

---

[104] 297 U. S. 284.

[105] *Ibid.,* 286.

[106] Failures to meet such technicalities of the law were apt to be due to the inexperience of lawyers assigned by courts for Negro defense.

[107] 297 U. S. 286.

[108] Accepting the decision as just, the *Daily Clarion-Ledger* (Jackson, Miss.), February 26, 1936, 7, deplored the fact that it gave Mississippi "some costly publicity and bad advertising." For comments as to the effects of the decision, see New York *Times,* February 21, 1936, 16 and Washington *Afro-American,* February 22, 1936, 1.

aspect in the case of *Chambers v. Florida.*[109] Whereas the method of coercion proscribed by the Court in *Brown v. Mississippi* was physical violence and brutality, the present case involved the use of repeated and protracted questioning in obtaining a confession. In May, 1933, Chambers and several other Negroes were arrested without warrants on suspicion of murder. After six days of protracted questioning, " they broke " and confessed to the crime. The confessions thus obtained were used in the trial which resulted in conviction and the death sentence. The Supreme Court of Florida upheld the lower court and appeal was made to the United States Supreme Court.

Justice Black read the opinion of the Court on February 12, 1940.[110] He first denied the state's contention that the Supreme Court was without jurisdiction and could not go behind the judgment of the state court and examine the facts. He asserted: " The use by the State of improperly obtained confessions may constitute a denial of due process under the Fourteenth Amendment . . . thus, we must determine independently whether the petitioners' confessions were so [improperly] obtained, by review of the facts upon which that issue necessarily turns." [111]

An examination of the facts revealed that, from the time the petitioners were arrested until sentenced to death, they were in the custody and under the influence of state officers whose " pressure " had resulted in their confessions. Pointing out that due process had its origin in the desire to protect " the poor, the ignorant, the friendless, and the penniless " from those in authority, Justice Black said:

> The determination to preserve an accused's right to procedural due process springs in large part from knowledge of the historic truth that the rights and liberties of people accused of crime could not be safely intrusted to secret inquisitorial processes. . . . The rack, the thumbscrew,

---

[109] 309 U. S. 227.

[110] A great deal of drama surrounded the reading of the opinion: it was read on Lincoln's Birthday; it protected the constitutional rights of Negroes; and it was read by Justice Hugo Black, whose appointment to the Supreme Court had been opposed by Negroes.

[111] 309 U. S. 229.

> the wheel, solitary confinement, protracted questioning and cross questioning, and other ingenious forms of entrapment of the helpless or unpopular had left their wake of mutilated bodies and shattered minds along the way to the cross, the guillotine, the stake, and the hangman's noose.[112]

The Court found that the confessions had been obtained " under circumstances calculated to break the strongest nerves and stoutest resistance." Though physical violence had not been resorted to, compulsion was nevertheless applied in the form of protracted questioning, thought Justice Black. The Court had no alternative but to reverse the judgment of the Supreme Court of Florida, for " to permit human lives to be forfeited upon confessions thus obtained would make of the constitutional requirement of due process of law a meaningless symbol." [113]

The decision in this case represents a unique application of the " due process " clause in such cases.[114] It refined due process to include mental, as well as physical, torture. Compulsion of this sort appears not to be unusual in cases involving Negroes in many southern states. To many Negroes and lovers of justice, it was heartening to hear Justice Black say: " Due process of law . . . commands that no practice such as that disclosed by this record shall send any accused to his death." [115] Less than a month after the decision in *Chambers v. Florida,* its rule was applied in the case of *Canty v. Alabama,* resulting in a *per curiam* decision.[116]

On May 27, 1940, Justice Black read an opinion denying a rehearing for Texas in a case closely paralleling the Florida tor-

---

[112] *Ibid.,* 238.

[113] *Ibid.,* 240. Commenting on the results of the decision, counsel for the Negro petitioners stated: " Florida Negroes regarded the pronouncement as a second Emancipation." *Crisis,* XLVII (1940), 84.

[114] It should be noted that this rule had already been pronounced by the Supreme Court of Tennessee in the case of *Rounds v. State,* 106 S. W. (2d) 212 (Tenn., 1937). On that occasion the court declared: " To deprive a human of sleep for four days and nights is a form of torture not less severe than physical violence . . . a confession so obtained is not admissible."

[115] 309 U. S. 241.

[116] *Ibid.,* 629.

ture case. The Court had handed down a *per curiam* decision in this case, *White v. Texas,*[117] under authority of the ruling in *Chambers v. Florida.* Texas petitioned for a rehearing on the ground that White, the Negro petitioner in the case, having denied making the confession used to convict him before the state court, could not contend before the Supreme Court that the use of the confession had denied him due process of law. The state was reminded by the Court that: "We must determine whether the record shows that . . . the confession was obtained and used in such a manner that the petitioner's trial fell short of that procedural due process guaranteed by the Constitution." [118] Having already determined that question in its *per curiam* decision in the case, the state's petition for rehearing was denied. Concluding the opinion in words almost identical to those in *Chambers v. Florida,* Justice Black asserted: "Due process of law, preserved for all by our Constitution, commands that no such practice as that disclosed by this record shall send any accused to his death." [119]

An effort was made to evade the rule of *Chambers v. Florida* in a case arising in Atlanta, Georgia, in 1940, and decided by a United States District Court. Quintar South, a Negro youth, was arrested on suspicion of theft. He alleged that Sutherland, the city detective who arrested him, violated his constitutional rights by extorting a confession from him through coercive means.[120] Admitting the alleged facts, counsel for Sutherland argued that the third-degree acts committed, being uncondoned by either state law or custom, were private acts and, therefore, did not fall within the "due process" clause of the Fourteenth Amendment. The Court thought otherwise and ruled that the coercive acts in question constituted state action in that they

---

[117] *Ibid.,* 631.

[118] 310 U. S. 532.

[119] *Ibid.* The case was remanded to the courts in Texas for retrial. During the trial, Bob White, the Negro defendant, was slain before the court by the husband of the woman who had accused him of rape.

[120] *United States v. Sutherland,* 37 Fed. Supp. 344. Pictures published the day after the arrest revealed the use of torture, including cigarette-burning.

had been committed by a state officer in the performance of his duty. Such action was prohibited by the Fourteenth Amendment.[121]

During 1941 and 1942, the issue of using coercive measures to secure confessions from Negroes accused of crime was before the United States Supreme Court in three cases. Two of these were determined by *per curiam* decisions applying the rule of *Chambers v. Florida*.[122] The decision in the third case was written by Justice Byrnes and read on June 1, 1942.[123] The case arose from the indictment and conviction of William Ward, a Negro citizen of Texas, for murder. The confession, allegedly voluntarily made, was the chief evidence in the conviction. Ward claimed that the confession was signed only after he had been seized without warrant, whipped, burned, and questioned continuously for three days. This action, he contended, was a violation of his rights under the "due process" clause.

The state appellate court contended that, under Texas criminal procedure, the question of admitting the confession in evidence was solely for the trial jury to decide. Justice Byrnes thought that such a question of state procedure should not stand in the way of the petitioner's constitutional right. He asserted that:

> Each state has the right to prescribe tests governing the admissibility of a confession. But when, as in the present case, the question is raised as to whether a defendant has been denied the due process of law guaranteed by the Federal Constitution, we cannot be precluded by the verdict of a jury from determining whether the circumstances under which the confession was made

---

[121] 37 Fed. Supp. 345.

[122] *Lomax v. Texas,* 313 U. S. 544 (1941); *Vernon v. Alabama,* 313 U. S. 547 (1941). The issue was also raised in the case of *Wilcoxon v. Aldridge,* 15 S. E. (2d) 873 (1941), before the Supreme Court of Georgia. In this instance the court ruled that the charge of coercion, having been made only after conviction, was not provable by the petitioner in habeas corpus proceedings and must be considered a waiver of the constitutional right involved. However, the charge of denial of right of counsel, which was also alleged, was sustained because this was "so fundamental an error that the whole trial was rendered illegal." 15 S. E. (2d) 877.

[123] *Ward v. Texas,* 316 U. S. 547.

> were such that its admission in evidence amounts to a denial of due process.[124]

An examination of the record seemed to support the conclusion that, in addition to acting without authority of the law, the arresting officers had coerced and intimidated the petitioner. The facts presented to the Court led Justice Byrnes to say: "We must conclude that this confession was not free and voluntary but was the product of coercion and duress, [and] that the petitioner was no longer able to freely admit or deny or to refuse to answer." [125] The use of a confession so obtained constituted a denial of due process of law, and the conviction could not stand.

This group of cases, successfully invoking the guarantees of the Fourteenth Amendment in criminal action in southern jurisdictions, seemed to forecast increased federal protection for Negroes accused of crime against arbitrary action by state officers. Maltreatment of the character involved in these litigations was brought within the scope of the limitations of the Fourteenth Amendment and declared a violation of due process of law. The willingness of the Supreme Court to apply this test of due process served to subject state criminal procedure to closer scrutiny.

During the period 1936–1943, the issue of the exclusion of Negroes from jury service was litigated along with that of convictions based on coerced confessions. There were four decisions by the Supreme Court on this issue during this period; and these decisions tended to extend the application of the "equal protection" clause beyond the application adopted in the second *Scottsboro* case. In the latter instance, the Court had ruled that the absence of Negroes from juries for an extended period was *prima facie* evidence of an unconstitutional discrimination.[126]

---

[124] *Ibid.*, 550.

[125] *Ibid.*, 555.

[126] The Supreme Court applied this rule in a *per curiam* decision in the case of *Hale v. Kentucky,* 303 U. S. 613 (1938). Holding the second Scottsboro ruling controlling, the Supreme Court of Missouri refused to let a case involving the question of the exclusion of Negroes from jury service "pass off" on a procedural technicality. See *State v. Logan,* 111 S. W. (2d) 113 (1937).

In the case of *Pierre v. Louisiana,*[127] decided February 27, 1939, Justice Black held that the rule of the second *Scottsboro* case applied to the grand jury and the trial jury alike. The case arose from the indictment and conviction of Pierre, a Negro, of murder. During the trial a motion was made to quash the indictment and the jury list from which both the grand and petit juries were drawn on the grounds of the unconstitutional exclusion of Negroes from jury service. The motion was sustained to quash the trial jury and the list from which it was drawn, but the indictment was allowed to stand though the grand jury was drawn from the same list as the trial jury. An appeal to the Supreme Court of Louisiana brought, in addition to an affirmation of the conviction, the ruling that the trial judge had erred in quashing the trial jury panel. It was held that the petitioner had not proved the exclusion of Negroes on account of race and color.[128]

A different conclusion was reached by the United States Supreme Court. Expressing great respect for the state court's judgment, Justice Black stated: "When a claim is properly asserted . . . that a citizen whose life is at stake has been denied the equal protection of his country's laws on account of his race, it becomes our solemn duty to make independent inquiry of the disputed facts."[129] The record showed that no Negroes had served on the grand jury in the parish, where the petitioner was convicted, for forty years; nor did it appear that their absence was due to a lack of statutory qualifications for jury service. More than half of the parish population was made up of Negroes, the majority of whom were literate and of good character. Moreover, the trial judge, who was familiar with local conditions, had ruled that there had been an unconstitutional discrimination against Negroes. This evidence "created a strong prima facie showing that negroes had been systematically excluded, because of race, from the Grand Jury," concluded Justice Black.[130] Since the principles which forbade discrimination in the selection of trial juries also apply to the grand jury, the Court

---

[127] 306 U. S. 354.

[128] *Ibid.*, 358.

[129] *Ibid.*

[130] *Ibid.*, 361.

ruled that the petitioner had been denied equal protection of the law and the state court's judgment was reversed.[131]

The calling of an occasional Negro to jury service was held insufficient to satisfy the demand of equal protection of law. This rule was established by the Supreme Court in 1940 in the case of *Smith v. Texas*.[132] It appears that this effort was made to evade the rule of the second *Scottsboro* case by Titus County, Texas. A Negro, convicted of rape by the courts of Texas, appealed to the United States Supreme Court alleging the systematic exclusion of Negroes from the jury which had indicted him on account of race.

Some unusual facts were brought to light by the Court's examination of the proof submitted by the petitioner. Negroes constituted ten to twenty per cent of the county population, and three to six thousand of them possessed the statutory qualifications for jury service. Of three hundred and eighty-four persons serving as grand jurors between 1931 and 1938, only five of these had been Negroes; and three of these five Negroes served three times. Eighteen Negroes had been summoned for jury service; however, on each such occasion, the Negro's name had been the last name on a sixteen-name jury list. The custom prevailed of selecting a twelve man jury in the order of the names on the list.[133]

Defining the use and composition of juries in a democratic society and their relationship to the Fourteenth Amendment, Justice Black stated:

> It is part of the established tradition in the use of juries as instruments of public justice that the jury be a body

---

[131] Local attorneys criticized the decision. One held that: "The United States Supreme Court simply disagreed with the Louisiana Supreme Court as to what the evidence proved." It was felt that since the Louisiana jury law directed the selection of "the best qualified" persons for jury service, it was necessary for those challenging jury lists to furnish a more positive proof of discrimination than if the selection were merely of persons meeting specified qualifications. See "Exclusion of Negroes from Juries," 1 *Louisiana Law Review,* 841–45; Betty Booth, "The Sufficiency of Evidence to Establish Discrimination," 30 *Journal of Criminal Law,* 264–66.

[132] 311 U. S. 128.

[133] *Ibid.*

> truly representative of the community. For a racial discrimination to result in the exclusion from jury service of otherwise qualified groups, not only violates our Constitution and the laws enacted under it, but is at war with our basic concepts of a democratic society and a representative government. . . . The fact that the written word of a state's laws holds out a promise that no discrimination be practiced is not enough. The Fourteenth Amendment requires that equal protection to all must be given—not merely promised.[134]

The Texas statute providing for the constitution of juries had given wide discretion to those responsible for the selection of jurors; and this discretion was capable of being exercised in such a manner as to exclude those groups deemed undesirable. That this had been done appeared obvious to Justice Black, for "chance and accident alone couldn't have brought about the listing of so few negroes from among thousands shown to have the qualifications, or invariably being listed as number sixteen and number sixteen never called for service."[135] The state's argument, that so few Negroes were chosen because the jury commissioners selected jurors from among their acquaintances and not being personally acquainted with Negroes, knew of none who had the necessary qualifications, was held inconclusive. "What the Fourteenth Amendment prohibits is racial discrimination in the selection of grand juries," declared Justice Black, and "where jury commissioners limit those from whom grand juries are selected to their own personal acquaintances, discrimination can arise from commissioners who know no negroes as well as from commissioners who know but eliminate them."[136] The Fourteenth Amendment forbade discrimination whether "ingeniously" or "ingenuously" accomplished. Evidence of unconstitutional discrimination was so evident that the conviction appealed from could not stand.

Two years after this ruling, an opportunity was presented for its application in the case of *Hill v. Texas*,[137] also decided by

[134] *Ibid.*, 130.

[135] *Ibid.*, 131.

[136] *Ibid.*, 132.

[137] 316 U. S. 400 (1942).

the United States Supreme Court. Here a Negro indicted for rape moved to quash his indictment on the grounds of a denial of equal protection of law in that Negroes were systematically excluded from the indicting jury. The motion was denied, and conviction followed. On appeal to the Court of Criminal Appeals of Texas, it was held that the petitioner offered only inference, not proof, that Negroes were discriminated against in the selection of juries.[138] Certiorari was granted by the United States Supreme Court to review this judgment.

The Supreme Court examined the evidence submitted by the Negro petitioner and found that the jury commissioner summoned only white persons for jury service. Moreover, according to their testimony, they neither knew nor attempted to find whether there were Negroes in the county with the necessary qualifications for jury service. Census statistics established the fact that there was a large number of literate Negroes in the county. In the face of these facts, Chief Justice Stone concluded: "We think the petitioner made out a prima facie case, which the state failed to meet, of racial discrimination in the selection of grand jurors."[139] The commissioners' failure to make an effort to discover whether or not there were qualified Negroes in the county was characterized as a "neglect of their constitutional duty."

Climaxing a tendency which was evident in the Court's rulings on the jury issue since the mid-thirties, Chief Justice Stone pointed out that the burden of proof to show lack of discrimination was on the state. The petitioner had presented evidence which inferred discrimination, he asserted, and:

> . . . we think here, that had there been evidence obtainable to contradict the inference . . . the State would not have refrained from introducing it, and the evidence which was introduced showed that there were colored citizens of the county qualified and available for jury service.[140]

---

[138] *Ibid.*

[139] *Ibid.*, 404.

[140] *Ibid.*

The state court's judgment was reversed because the state had failed to afford the petitioner that equal protection of the law which the Fourteenth Amendment commands.

A comparison of the opinions in the two jury cases, *Smith v. Texas* and *Hill v. Texas,* brings to view some significant observations. The opinions, written by Justice Black and Chief Justice Stone respectively, nullified discriminatory practices of a state of the deep-South. Moreover, with the possible exception of the two opinions of Justice Holmes in *Moore v. Dempsey* and *Nixon v. Herndon,* these two opinions were more caustic and censorious than any opinion handed down by the Supreme Court in a case involving a Negro issue during the entire period since 1920.[141] Perhaps in no decision of the Court, which involved the Negro, can there be found a more forceful exposition of the purpose of the Fourteenth Amendment and the duty of the Supreme Court under that amendment than in these two opinions on the jury issue.

There was an interesting use of statistics by the Supreme Court of South Carolina, in 1942, to prove the non-existence of Negroes qualified for jury service. In the case of *Grant v. State,*[142] decided three weeks before the case of *Hill v. Texas,* a Negro convicted of murder alleged that Negroes had been unconstitutionally excluded from the jury which indicted him. The court, in meeting this allegation, pointed out that jurors were required to be registered electors according to the law of South Carolina. Registration statistics for Berkeley County, where the case arose, established the fact that only one Negro had registered or attempted to register in the two and a half year period preceding the trial. Therefore, there was only one Negro in the County

---

[141] The fact that one of these opinions was written by Justice Black of Alabama seems to substantiate the obvious conclusion of Cortez A. M. Ewing, *Judges of the Supreme Court, 1789–1937,* 7, that "each general geographical section embraces men of every shade of political opinion. One cannot assume, therefore, that a southern-derived judge represents the South any more than he reflects the ideas of New England or the Pacific Coast." Presumably, this would hold for any people, race, nationality, or creed.

[142] 19 S. E. (2d) 638.

who was eligible for jury service. The court could but conclude that: "It is the failure of members of the Negro race in Berkeley County to exercise their rights under the constitution, rather than any act of the State or its administrative officials, which accounts for the absence from the jury list of all members of that race except one in that County."[143] The South Carolina jury law illustrates the effectiveness of employing the electoral qualification as an instrument of exclusion.

The position taken by the United States Supreme Court on the question of the exclusion of Negroes from jury service between 1936 and 1943 did much to extend legal protection against this type of discrimination.[144] Rigid application of the rules established by the Supreme Court on this matter was urged upon the senior Circuit Court Judges of the United States in 1942. They were cautioned that:

> Anything that amounts to a conscious and deliberate exclusion from jury lists of any class of persons solely on account of race, color, economic or social status is improper and may be unlawful . . . [no] jury panel can be regarded as secure from challenge unless there has been an earnest effort on the part of the court, the clerk, and the jury commissioners to assure that there is no discrimination against these groups.[145]

As far as legal interpretation was concerned, evasive argument and claims of lack of discriminatory intent could no longer refute the allegation of unconstitutional discrimination against Negroes in the constitution of juries.[146]

---

[143] *Ibid.*, 641.

[144] Bernard S. Jefferson, "Race Discrimination in Jury Service," 19 *Boston University Law Review,* 447, holds that the Supreme Court's early failure to declare its right to supervise the state judicial system was responsible for the consumption of so much time and effort in the attempt to prevent the selection of racially biased jurors.

[145] Conference of the Chief Justice with the Senior Circuit Court Judges of the United States, *Report of the Committee on Selection of Juries,* September 8, 1942, quoted in *United States* ex rel. *Jackson v. Brady,* 132 Fed. (2d) 479.

[146] However, the courts still insisted that charges of exclusion be both adequately raised during trial and supported by some proof. See *Car-*

Nevertheless, the problem has not been entirely solved. There is much evidence that many southern jurisdictions have not been too diligent in applying the rules established by the Supreme Court on the jury issue.[147] The results of a survey made in 1940 suggest that while Negroes usually served on federal juries in the South, they were still largely excluded from jury service in state courts, except in a few of the larger cities.[148] It appears that serious consideration is given Negroes, in regard to jury service, only in cases where appeal is imminent. Practice seemed to refute the opinion of a southern editor who stated: "There are few even so called practical objections to service by Negroes on the jury." [149]

Though unrelated to the jury issue, the decision in the case of *Mitchell v. United States,*[150] decided April 28, 1941, called attention to a constitutional issue upon which there had been practically no litigation since 1920—the segregation of Negro interstate passengers.[151] The case arose from the fact that Representative Arthur W. Mitchell, a Negro and Democratic member of Congress from Chicago, was compelled to move from a Pullman compartment into a "colored coach" in conformity with the segregation laws of Arkansas. An appeal before the Interstate Commerce Commission, charging denial of equal treatment, resulted in the ruling that the treatment received was neither "unjust nor undue" because the slight demand for first-class services by Negro passengers made the running of extra trains unwar-

ruthers v. Reed, 102 Fed. (2d) 933 (C.C.A. 8th Ct., Ark. [1939]); *United States* ex rel. *Jackson v. Brady,* 132 Fed. (2d) 476 (C.C.A. 4th Ct., Md. [1943]).

[147] Washington *Afro-American,* March 10, 1940, 3; Chicago, *Defender,* October 16, 1943, 2, 5; Pittsburgh *Courier,* January 29, 1944, 2.

[148] Gunnar Myrdal, *An American Dilemma,* I, 549 f.

[149] Dallas *Morning News,* June 2, 1942, II, 4.

[150] 313 U. S. 80. It should be noted that this case, arising under the Interstate Commerce Act, was decided by application of the "equal protection" clause of the Fourteenth Amendment.

[151] See *South Covington and Cinn. Ry. v. Commonwealth,* 205 S. W. 633 (Ky., 1920) and *Chiles v. Chesapeake and Ohio Ry. Co.,* 218 U. S. 71 (1914). In the latter case the Supreme Court held that where there was no state statute attempting to regulate interstate commerce in the matter, the act of a private company in establishing reasonable rules and regulations could not be constrained.

ranted. The United States Supreme Court granted appeal to review this judgment.

Both Negroes and southern state officials revealed great interest in the case. In action considered unprecedented, the attorneys-general of ten southern states urged the Supreme Court not to pass upon the constitutionality of the segregation law of Arkansas.[152] They felt that the question was such a sensitive one that the Federal courts should not interfere unless there was no alternative.

To the contention advanced by Representative Mitchell before the Supreme Court of unequal treatment, counsel for the Interstate Commerce Commission held that the Interstate Commerce Act neither required nor prohibited segregation. Furthermore, the Commission was acting within its authority in refusing to issue an order requiring an interstate carrier to provide permanent facilities for which there was such small demand.[153] Meeting this argument, Chief Justice Hughes said: "He [Mitchell] is an American citizen, free to travel and he is entitled to go by this particular route whenever he chooses to take it and he is entitled to have facilities for his journey without any discrimination which the Interstate Commerce Act forbids." [154]

The Interstate Commerce Commission contended that segregation was the long-established policy in Arkansas and that it was supported by earlier opinions of the Supreme Court. But there was an essential difference between the cases in which such rules were established and the case under review, the Court pointed out. Here "the question is one of equality of treatment and not a question of segregation." Moreover, "the denial of equality of accommodations because of his race would be an invasion of a fundamental right which is guaranteed against state action by

---

[152] Washington *Afro-American,* May 7, 1941, 1. An editorial, "Negroes Are People," *New Republic,* CIV (1941), 616–17, suggested that southern leaders offered a compromise of support of large federal grants of money for Negro education in the South if the Supreme Court would not demand equality of treatment for Negroes and whites on interstate trains. "But one does not bargain with the Supreme Court," concluded the editorial.

[153] 313 U. S. 84, 85.

[154] *Ibid.,* 93.

the Fourteenth Amendment."[155] Colored passengers, who purchase first-class tickets, must be furnished with accommodations equal to those provided for white passengers, the Court concluded. Forcing a Negro interstate passenger, who had purchased a first-class ticket, into a second-class coach because he was a Negro was discriminatory treatment in that it denied him the standard privileges and conveniences afforded first-class white passengers.[156] The Chief Justice concluded the opinion with the assertion that:

> The comparative volume of traffic cannot justify the denial of a fundamental right of equality of treatment. . . . It is the individual . . . , who is entitled to the equal protection of the laws, not merely a group of individuals, or a body of persons according to their numbers. If facilities are provided at all, substantial equality of persons traveling under like conditions cannot be refused.[157]

The case was remanded to the United States District Court to set aside the Commission's ruling sustaining the practice of unequal treatment.

Coming so recently, it is impossible to estimate the practical results of the ruling in *Mitchell v. United States.* The case did have the effect of publicizing the conditions under which Negro passengers are compelled to travel in and through states where the races are separated by statutory mandate.[158] While some persons held that the immediate result of the decision would be the provision of better accommodations for Negro interstate passengers,[159] it should be kept in mind that the decision neither invalidated racial segregation in interstate commerce, nor did it demand identical accommodations for Negro passengers. The doctrine of "substantial equality," long applied in litigation on

---

155 *Ibid.*

156 *Ibid.*, 95. While the litigation was in process, the Interstate Commerce Commission ordered interstate carriers to provide equal facilities for Negro interstate passengers.

157 313 U. S. 97.

158 Charles S. Mangum, *The Legal Status of Negroes,* 221–22.

159 New York *Sun,* April 29, 1941, 20; New York *Herald-Tribune,* April 29, 1941, 1, 12; Washington *Afro-American,* May 3, 1941, 1, 13.

the issue of racial segregation, was maintained here. But "the Supreme Court's ruling is half a loaf," remarked one editor, "it is better than no bread." [160] Substantially equal accommodations for Negro interstate passengers, though segregated, were considered an improvement over conditions and facilities which had prevailed. There is great possibility that further exploitation of this question by Negroes, encouraged by the Court's ruling in the *Mitchell* case, will result in a large amount of litigation on the issue.[161]

A statistical study of cases involving the Fourteenth Amendment and the Negro between 1936 and 1943 indicates the continuation of many trends observed in the two earlier periods treated. During this period, thirty-two decisions were handed down by American courts in litigation of this character. Twenty-six of the total number of cases were determined at the appellate level and distributed as follows: the United States Supreme Court, fifteen cases; [162] United States Circuit Court of Appeals, three cases; and state courts of last resort, eight cases. Ten of the fifteen cases decided by the Supreme Court during this period were concentrated in the two year period, 1940–1942. Moreover, all of these decisions were favorable to the Negro petitioners.[163] Decisions favorable to the Negro interest involved were handed down in twenty-six out of thirty-two cases.[164]

There is evidence that the liberal tendencies observed in the Supreme Court between 1931 and 1936 had become prevailing

---

[160] Washington *Afro-American,* May 10, 1941, 4.

[161] See Frank E. Quindry, "Airline Passenger Discrimination," 3 *Journal of Air Law,* 479–514, for a discussion of the issue as it relates to airline passengers. There are no "jim crow" statutes applying directly to airlines; thus, it appears that airlines may or may not separate passengers according to race. But it would seem that where segregation is adopted, equality of treatment must be accorded.

[162] Four of these decisions were written by Justice Hugo Black of Alabama and one by Justice James Byrnes of South Carolina; all five were favorable to the Negro interest involved.

[163] See Appendix.

[164] Gordon B. Hancock, editorial, Norfolk *Journal and Guide,* January 7, 1939, 6, concluded that these liberal tendencies were but the reflection of President Roosevelt's liberal attitudes and policies.

practices in the later years of the period 1936–1943.[165] The increased number of instances of review of state court judgments by the Supreme Court suggests a movement away from the Court's earlier position of leaving problems affecting relations between the races to the discretion of the states. Placing a greater emphasis upon "the fundamental constitutional rights of the citizen," an independent examination of facts by the Supreme Court became the usual procedure. The phrase, "we must determine independently," occupied a prominent place in the Court's opinions during this period. Moreover, in such cases as *Pierre v. Louisiana, Smith v. Texas, Hill v. Texas,* and *Ward v. Texas,* the decisions turned upon the fact that the Supreme Court went behind the record and examined and interpreted the facts for itself. Thus, Justice Holmes' doctrine of "cutting beneath the record" was finally adopted after almost two decades of hesitation. Despite objections on the part of the states to the practice, there were repeated assertions of the Court's duty to measure the states' actions by the constitutional tests of due process and equal protection.

Due process and equal protection of law were both more broadly interpreted and applied after 1936, in regard to litigation involving the Negro, than at any other time in the history of the Supreme Court. Due process, as defined in cases dealing with coerced confessions, was broadened by the addition of another essential element—the freedom of the citizen from the application of compulsion in any form, whether physical or mental, in criminal action directed against him.

The Court's interpretation of equal protection was likewise broadened. Decisions applying this clause of the Fourteenth Amendment tended to make it something more than a mere slogan. The doctrine of "substantial equality" was maintained throughout this period.[166] But the earlier interpretation of the

---

[165] Editorial, Washington *Afro-American,* January 13, 1943, 4, urged that the separation of races in any form was an abridgement of Negroes' rights under the Fourteenth Amendment and suggested that the question be put to "our present liberal Supreme Court."

[166] Kievets, *loc. cit.,* 75. "The Legality of Race Segregation in Educational Opportunities," 82 *University of Pennsylvania Law Review,* 164.

doctrine, which invariably held that almost any facility provided by the state for its Negro citizens met the test of " substantial equality," gave way to an effort to appraise more fairly the privileges and facilities afforded each race. This departure is most apparent in the *Gaines* and *Mitchell* cases. Despite some opinion to the contrary, these two cases seem to indicate that the Supreme Court has " whittled " the doctrine of substantial equality and made of the " equal protection " clause " a command which the State must respect, the benefits of which every person may demand." [167]

One factor, commonly considered the chief difficulty in enforcing the Fourteenth Amendment in criminal cases involving Negroes, was the Supreme Court's cautious reluctance in assuming jurisdiction in cases where conflict with state criminal procedure was apparent.[168] This practice tended to leave the constitutional rights of Negro citizens under the sole protection of state courts. Commenting on this policy, one writer states.

> Had the Supreme Court properly and liberally interpreted the legislation designed to protect the civil rights of the Negro and enforce the guarantees and immunities of the Fourteenth Amendment, there would have been acceptance of the supervisory control of the federal courts over the judicial system, just as there has been acceptance of federal judicial control over state legislation. . . . The Supreme Court must withdraw from its collaboration in the partial nullification of the Fourteenth Amendment and assume a broader view of its protective function.[169]

The facts seem to indicate that the Supreme Court has been less hesitant in this respect since 1940 than ever before. At least six of the decisions handed down by the Court between 1940 and 1943, in litigation involving the Negro, concerned questions of state criminal procedure. The Court has recently been emphatic in its declaration that, in applying the provisions of the Four-

---

[167] *Hill v. Texas,* 316 U. S. 406; also 6 *University of Chicago Law Review,* 305.

[168] *Supra,* 45–46.

[169] Jefferson, *loc. cit.,* 447.

teenth Amendment, it would not be bound by considerations of state criminal procedure or its technicalities.[170]

Whether or not the nation as a whole was conscious of the fact, between 1936 and 1943 the Supreme Court was following a new path in applying the Fourteenth Amendment in matters affecting the Negro. Only a careful reading of the Court's opinions can fully demonstrate how far the Court had gone along the pathway of liberal interpretation and broad application of the amendment. There is much assurance that the end result will be a fuller protection of human rights and the extension of fuller rights of American citizenship to Negroes.

---

[170] See *Ward v. Texas,* 316 U. S. 547; *Brown v. Mississippi,* 297 U. S. 286.

CHAPTER V

AN ACCOUNTING AND A CONCLUSION

Though the wisdom of the passage of the Fourteenth Amendment has been questioned many times, its principal purpose, to confer additional rights and privileges upon members of the recently emancipated Negro race, appeared a logical step in the development of the theory of American democracy as defined in the late eighteenth century. Commented Senator Howard of Michigan in 1866:

> The great object of the first section of this amendment is . . . to restrain the power of the States and compel them at all times to respect these great fundamental guarantees. . . . The last two clauses of the first section of the amendment disable a State from depriving not merely a citizen of the United States, but any person whatever, whoever he may be, of life, liberty, or property without due process of law, or from denying to him the equal protection of the laws of the State. This abolishes all class legislation in the States and does away with the injustice of subjecting one caste of persons to a code not applicable to the other.[1]

This was the great purpose of the amendment which, if realized, would extend citizenship to the American Negro and protect him in the exercise of its rights and privileges. Congress felt that the Fourteenth Amendment, as passed, granted sufficient power to the Federal Government to implement the purpose for which this amendment was drawn up. However, the history of the Fourteenth Amendment, as it has applied to the Negro, demonstrates the wide gulf between real and romantic democracy. It further demonstrates that the great purpose of the framers has not even been approximated, except perhaps during the past eight years.

[1] Quoted in William D. Guthrie, *The Fourteenth Article of Amendment to the Constitution of the United States,* 22–23.

Unfortunately, problems of Negro citizenship and rights have been inextricably bound up with questions of national racial policy and sectional racial tradition. These considerations, more than is sometimes realized, have determined that the immunities and guarantees of the Fourteenth Amendment be partially extended to the Negro only slowly and after a great deal of litigation before the courts. Such guarantees as have been extended fall far short of the congressional ideal of 1866. One writer has contended that there are, in reality, two Fourteenth Amendments: the first is the amendment as it came from the hand of the framers; the second, the amendment as it has been written and rewritten by the Supreme Court in its numerous decisions involving an interpretation of the amendment since 1873.[2] That the "two Amendments" differ widely from one another admits of no questioning. Prior to 1935, the narrow construction and application of the Fourteenth Amendment in cases involving racial matters so limited the rights and privileges of the Negro that many persons were convinced that the Fourteenth Amendment had failed in its results. As late as 1939, one attorney said: "Some feel that the court could have wielded a great moral and educative force; or at least refrained from lending moral support to continued inequalities heaped upon the Negro." [3]

During the twenties and early thirties, the manner in which the Fourteenth Amendment was interpreted and applied by the Supreme Court suggested that not too much was being done to fulfill the original purpose of the amendment. No one of the three clauses of the first section of the amendment—and these in effect are the amendment—was broadly enough interpreted or applied to extend to Negroes the fundamental rights of citizenship. The Court determined that there were few privileges and immunities accruing to United States citizenship as against state citizenship; it determined due process of law in such a manner as to give the suggestion that state criminal procedure had a sacrosanct character; it held that equal protection of the law

[2] F. Lyman Windolph, "Two Fourteenth Amendments," *Annals of the Academy of Political and Social Science,* CVC (1939), 277.

[3] "The Negro Citizen in the Supreme Court," 52 *Harvard Law Review,* 832. See also 20 *Minnesota Law Review,* 673.

was afforded by the states when "similar" provisions or opportunities were extended to minority peoples. These interpretations all but emasculated the "privileges and immunities" clause and confined the other two to such narrow limits that Negroes complained that the Supreme Court sometimes appeared to place a higher regard upon states' rights than upon human rights.[4]

The narrow construction given the Fourteenth Amendment by the Court, as it applied to the Negro, is fully understood only when that construction is related to the prevailing sentiment of the period. If it is true that "half of the Constitution is what the Fourteenth Amendment is,"[5] it is equally true that, in the final analysis, the Fourteenth Amendment is only what the American people want it to be. From this point of view, the amendment stands as a "charter of liberties" in protection of the rights of every American citizen or it becomes only an imperfect instrument for that purpose as the public will dictates. Court opinions are not produced in a social void; they are largely the product and reflection of the popular will and can extend or restrict rights and privileges to minority groups only as the majority opinion wills it. "Courts," declared one educator, "possibly without being aware of it, are always amenable to the influence of surrounding public opinion; . . . law is [more than] grinding out decisions independent of time, place, and conditions."[6] In many areas, the dependence of local judges upon the populace for re-election has sometimes led to partial justice for the Negro and other minorities and a disregard for their constitutional rights through the incorporation of local prejudices into court decisions.

If the Supreme Court's interpretation of the Fourteenth Amendment in cases regarding the Negro was conservative and restrictive during most of the period 1920–1943, it was because public

---

[4] Washington *Afro-American,* April 15, 1944, 4.

[5] Louis B. Boudin, "Truth and Fiction About the Fourteenth Amendment," 10 *New York University Law Quarterly Review,* 19.

[6] William H. Kilpatrick, "Resort to Courts by Negroes to Improve Their Schools is a Conditional Alternative," *Journal of Negro Education,* IV (1935), 317; also Ralph J. Bunche, "Tactics and Programs of Minority Groups," *Journal of Negro Education,* IV (1935), 315 f.

opinion supported that construction and that application of the amendment. Moreover, the Justices reflected an education and a background based upon that public concept of minorities and their limited rights. Thus, the Court's cautiousness in interfering with state criminal procedure, its tendency to leave matters affecting race relations to the states, and its unsatisfactory application of the rule of equal protection were all ideas to which popular opinion heartily subscribed.

Court opinions have little value in themselves. While they establish a body of legal precedents, opinions are valuable to minority groups only to the extent that they result in the actual protection and exercise of fundamental constitutional rights. It seems most improbable that, had the Supreme Court extended broad rights and privileges to Negroes under the Fourteenth Amendment during the early years of the period 1920–1943, public opinion would have permitted them to exercise such rights. The difficulty experienced in enforcing such decisions as those in *Norris v. Alabama* and *Missouri* ex rel. *Gaines v. Canada,* both of which involved an extension of constitutional rights to Negroes in disregard of public sentiment, seems to substantiate this fact. Abnormal reactions resulting from the post-war and depression eras, together with traditional American racial attitudes, discouraged any effort for a rapid enlargement of the Negro's privileges of citizenship.[7]

With few exceptions between 1920 and 1933, the application of the Fourteenth Amendment was conservative, and it resulted in few practical gains for Negroes. The Supreme Court "was no great friend of the black man" during this period, observed one writer.[8] Since 1935, however, the Supreme Court has revealed a persistent tendency to turn the Fourteenth Amendment back toward its original purpose—the protection of the Negro's constitutional rights. This tendency was manifested by a broader

---

[7] Donald Young, *Minority Peoples in the Depression,* 60–67; Charles S. Mangum, *The Legal Status of the Negro,* 173; United States Office of Education, *National Survey of Higher Education for Negroes,* I, 3–18, *passim.*

[8] "The Negro Citizen in the Supreme Court," 52 *Harvard Law Review,* 828.

and more liberal application of this amendment in litigation involving Negroes; by less concern over giving offense to those who subscribed to the states' rights philosophy; and by close examination of the intent and effect of state legislation affecting Negroes. Such tendencies resurrected the Fourteenth Amendment as an instrument for the protection of the Negro in the exercise of the fundamental privileges of American citizenship. The large percentage of favorable decisions by the Court on matters affecting the Negro since 1936 was indicative of a trend—a trend which will perhaps result in the extension of more complete rights of citizenship to Negroes.[9] The evidence leads to the conclusion that this trend, in recent years, has been both sustained and accelerated as much by the growth of a national interest in problems of minority peoples as by Supreme Court decisions. Without doubt, the former has made the latter possible. In the view of one writer, this trend "cannot be stopped by one state or by several states. It can be stopped only by a majority of the people of the United States." [10]

In the period after 1920, as before, the Negro was compelled to rely largely upon court litigation to gain the enjoyment of the guarantees and privileges set forth in the Fourteenth Amendment. The slowness of public opinion, particularly in the South where the vast majority of Negroes lived, in according the exercise of citizenship rights to Negroes resulted in the adoption of a broad program of legal action as the most effective means of securing those rights. Every opportunity was sought to contest instances of discrimination or unequal treatment of Negroes. The adoption of this approach to the problem necessarily resulted in an ever increasing amount of litigation in both state and Federal courts involving the Fourteenth Amendment and the Negro. Much of this litigation was concentrated in the period after 1936.

---

[9] Howard W. Odum, "Crisis in the Making," *Crisis*, L (1943), 360–62; Gunnar Myrdal, *An American Dilemma*, I, 516.

[10] "Sense and Nonsense from South Carolina," *Crisis*, XLVIII (1941), 287. For an illustration of the work being done in regard to increasing opportunities for minorities, see Edwin R. Embree, *Julius Rosenwald Fund, 1942–1944*, 16–20.

Of sixty nine cases decided in all courts between 1920 and 1943,[11] which involved the Fourteenth Amendment and the Negro, thirty-two cases or 46 per cent were concentrated in the seven year period, 1936–1943.

Two factors seem to explain the increase in litigation involving the Fourteenth Amendment and the Negro—a consciousness of unequal status in American society and organized effort on the part of Negroes. Increased educational opportunities brought to Negroes an awareness of the discriminatory treatment accorded them in some sections of the country. This awareness, before the end of the twenties, was translated into the desire—even demand—for participation in American life on an equal basis with other citizens. Non-segregated treatment was demanded, for Negroes were convinced, and it was too often demonstrated by fact, that segregated treatment was unequal treatment. Recognition of constitutional rights, many Negroes felt, could be attained only to the extent that Negroes organized their efforts and brought such issues before the courts for decision.

It was fortunate in this respect that the twenties was a decade in which Negroes placed emphasis upon racial solidarity and race pride. From the combination of race pride and consciousness of unequal treatment, there were evidences of greater cooperation among Negroes after 1930 than ever before. Cooperation and organized effort, exercised through a large number of Negro organizations, were directed toward the end of winning legal victories involving fundamental questions affecting Negro rights. "Legal victories," one Negro leader said, "as they can be and are used for propaganda purposes to educate the public, are no longer mere sentiment or agitation. They represent advances as concrete as any that can possibly be made in this work. Their effort is definitely measurable in the field of social relations."[12]

[11] This number does not include the large number of memorandum decisions or consent decrees handed down, especially after 1936, or cases involving other minority peoples, though the issue might have affected or possessed implications for Negro rights.

[12] Statement of James W. Johnson, Executive Secretary of the National Association for the Advancement of Colored People, to the annual convention of the Association in 1926, N.A.A.C.P., *Seventeenth Annual Report,* 1926, 5.

On some occasions Negroes were criticized by the Negro press for not contributing more effort and financial support to the program of legal action.[13]

The intensification of the Negro's campaign of legal action under the Fourteenth Amendment was suggested by an increase in the number of cases appealed, as well as an increase in the number of actions initiated. In each of the three periods of this study, there is evidence that an increasingly large percentage of cases was finally determined at the appellate level. Most striking of all in this respect is the large number of cases presented to the United States Supreme Court for decision. Between 1920 and 1943, the Supreme Court handed down twenty-seven decisions involving the Fourteenth Amendment and the Negro. Divided according to period they were as follows: 1920–1930, five decisions; 1931–1935, seven decisions; and 1936–1943, fifteen decisions. From this distribution of Supreme Court decisions, one can conclude that since 1920, Negroes have looked more and more to the Supreme Court, especially as it was liberally constituted in the late thirties, for the protection of their constitutional rights.

The number of decisions favorable to the Negro litigant in cases decided under the Fourteenth Amendment between 1920 and 1943 is impressive. Forty-five or 69.9 per cent of the sixty-nine decisions handed down by all courts were favorable to the Negro interests involved. After 1930, the percentage of favorable decisions tended to increase sharply. Whereas six of eighteen or only 33 per cent of the decisions handed down between 1920 and 1930 were favorable to the Negro litigant, eleven of nineteen or 42 per cent of the decisions between 1931 and 1935 and twenty-six of thirty-two or 75 per cent of the decisions between 1936 and 1943 were favorable to the Negro litigant.

Perhaps the most impressive percentage of legal victories was that in cases before the United States Supreme Court. Only two of twenty-seven or 7.4 per cent of the decisions handed down by that Court during the entire period, 1920–1943, were unfavorable to the Negro litigant. These two unfavorable decisions were

[13] Washington *Afro-American,* April 15, 1944, 1; also issue for March 1, 1941, 4.

Corrigan v. Buckley in 1926,[14] which involved the question of restrictive covenants, and *Grovey v. Townsend* in 1935,[15] which involved the question of the exclusion of Negroes from the Democratic primary in Texas. It should be noted, however, that the ruling in *Grovey v. Townsend* was reversed by the ruling in *Smith v. Allwright* in 1944,[16] decided under the Fifteenth Amendment. Thus, in the past nine years, no case brought before the Supreme Court under the Fourteenth Amendment by Negroes has been lost.

Undoubtedly, many factors explain the progressive increase in the percentage of legal victories won by Negroes before American courts under the Fourteenth Amendment during the period 1920–1943. Of great significance in this respect have been such factors as an improvement in race relations, the growth of a spirit of tolerance toward minorities by sections and elements of the people at large, especially in the late thirties, and the liberal tendencies observable in the Supreme Court during the later years of this period. No doubt all three factors contributed much to the final result. Another factor sometimes overlooked is the contribution of the Negro lawyer. Cases carried to the Supreme Court prior to 1920 represented the work of an occasional white attorney in the South rather than Negro effort.[17] There were few Negro lawyers in the South where most of the cases arose and where the need for legal action to protect the constitutional rights of Negroes was greatest.[18] And even sympathetic white lawyers, for both social and professional reasons, could not wage a consistent battle for the protection of the rights of Negroes.

During the early twenties, effort was concentrated upon developing a staff of competent Negro lawyers to fight cases of discriminatory treatment against Negroes before the courts. The

[14] 271 U. S. 323.

[15] 295 U. S. 45.

[16] 321 U. S. 649.

[17] Charles W. Collins, *The Fourteenth Amendment and the States,* 74–75.

[18] Charles H. Houston, "The Need for Negro Lawyers," *Journal of Negro Education,* IV (1935), 49–51, points out that there were only 1230 Negro lawyers in the entire United States in 1930 of which number only 487 were in the South. Only 100 of the 487 Negro lawyers in the South were devoted to full-time practice of the law.

efforts of the National Association for the Advancement of Colored People and the National Bar Association, an association of Negro lawyers, to develop a staff of competent Negro lawyers for this work have been commendable. These two organizations have worked closely together in crusading for the protection of Negroes' rights.[19] Negro lawyers, in the face of hostile public sentiment, argued cases involving Negro rights before both Federal and state courts in the South. Since the late twenties, the large majority of cases before the Supreme Court, which involved the Fourteenth Amendment and the Negro, were argued by Negro attorneys, who were members of or associated with the legal staff of the National Association for the Advancement of Colored People. The *United States Reports* show that the large majority of cases decided since 1935 were argued by Attorneys Thurgood Marshall, Charles H. Houston, Leon Ransom, William Hastie, and Robert Ming, all of whom were members of the legal staff of the National Association for the Advancement of Colored People.[20]

To a great extent, it appears that one reason for the great increase in the number of legal victories for Negroes before the courts after 1930 was better prepared cases and arguments than had prevailed before that time. Negro counsel had an interest in the outcome of cases over and above that of professional interest. The success of the Negro lawyer in the fight against the disregard of Negroes' constitutional rights caused one Negro editor to remark: "Maybe we should chuck the democratic and Christian wailers, beggars, and appeasers, and concentrate on hiring lawyers and keeping them in the courts fighting our battles there."[21] The answer to the problem of ending unconstitutional discrimination was to provide lawyers to contest more cases of such discrimination.

---

[19] Raymond P. Alexander, "The National Bar Association—Its Aims and Its Purpose," 1 *National Bar Journal,* 4, 5.

[20] Judge Hastie and Attorneys Ransom and Ming are members of the faculty of the Law School of Howard University. Attorney Houston is, at present, a member of the President's Committee on Fair Employment Practices.

[21] Washington *Afro-American,* March 1, 1944, 4.

A study of litigation involving the Fourteenth Amendment and the Negro since 1920 leads to some significant conclusions in regard to the subject-areas litigated. One issue consistently litigated during the entire period was that of protecting the constitutional rights of Negroes in criminal cases before southern courts. Different aspects of the issue litigated were mob-dominated trials, denial of right of counsel, the exclusion of Negroes from juries, and convictions based upon coerced confessions. While the jury question was under litigation during the entire period, the period after 1936 saw the greater emphasis placed upon contesting convictions of Negro defendants based upon coerced confessions. Seventeen of thirty-two cases decided between 1936 and 1943 involved the two issues of the exclusion of Negroes from jury service and the use of coerced confessions in securing convictions of Negroes in criminal cases.

Second in number only to cases involving questions of state criminal procedure were those dealing with the validity of action resulting in the exclusion of Negroes from the Democratic primary in southern states. Litigation on this question was concentrated in the period prior to 1935. There were six decisions on this issue between 1920 and 1930 and six between 1931 and 1935. The apparent finality of the decision in the case of *Grovey v. Townsend* in 1935 tended to discourage further litigation on the question.

Social questions litigated under the Fourteenth Amendment by Negroes between 1920 and 1943 centered around the two subjects of residential segregation and equal educational opportunities. The decade of the twenties saw a great deal of litigation on the question of the validity of segregation ordinances and restrictive covenants. Nine of the eighteen cases decided between 1920 and 1930 involved this question. The decision in the case of *Corrigan v. Buckley* in 1926, upholding the validity of restrictive covenants, and the decision in the case of *City of Richmond v. Deans* in 1930,[22] invalidating segregation ordinances, tended to discourage further court action on the subject by either whites or

[22] 281 U. S. 704.

Negroes. Only four decisions were found on the question in the years 1931–1943.

The question of gaining educational opportunities for Negroes has long been considered one of the fundamental problems affecting the status and advancement of the Negro race. It is, therefore, not surprising to find that a considerable amount of the effort spent to secure the enforcement of the Fourteenth Amendment centered around this question. In each of the three periods studied, there was at least one decision on the issue of the validity of racial classification for purposes of education; all of these were unfavorable to the Negro litigant. Failing to secure the invalidation of state statutes providing for separate schools, Negroes made a concerted effort to secure for Negroes in the South educational opportunities equal to those provided for white students. After 1935, much of the total legal effort was directed toward that end. Seven of the thirty-two or 21.9 per cent of the total number of decisions handed down between 1936 and 1943 involved some aspect of the question of equal educational opportunities for Negroes. An analysis of the subject-area distribution of decisions involving the Fourteenth Amendment and the Negro since 1920 leads to the conclusion that Negroes have been primarily interested in enforcing the Fourteenth Amendment as it relates to criminal action involving Negroes, matters of residence and suffrage, and questions affecting educational opportunities and facilities for Negroes in the South.[23]

Uniform treatment has not been accorded questions of discriminatory treatment of Negroes in Supreme Court decisions. Between 1920 and 1943, the decisions show conclusively that Negroes have been most successful in invoking the Fourteenth Amendment in cases involving questions of state criminal procedure and the treatment of Negroes suspected of crime. Litigation involving residential segregation by legislative enactment was also generally decided in favor of the Negro litigant as was that involving the exclusion of Negroes from participation in

---

[23] See Charles W. Collins, *The Fourteenth Amendment and the States,* 63–66, for a comparison with subject-area distribution of litigation between 1873 and 1910.

Democratic primaries in southern states. Among the least successful subject-areas litigated were segregation in public carriers and schools. It would seem from this evidence that the Court has generally invalidated racial classification in political and economic matters but has tended to support such classification in social matters,[24] whenever " substantially equal " provisions were made for Negroes. One writer concluded that: " In many ways the Supreme Court has been a bulwark of liberty, but its record in cases involving the claims of Negroes to the protection of the Constitution is scarcely one of which the Court—or we—can be proud." [25]

There has been little agreement as to the practical benefits of litigation under the Fourteenth Amendment in regard to the protection of the Negro's rights and privileges. At one extreme is that opinion which held that legal victories result in little practical benefit to the Negro; [26] at the other, the belief that legal victories " must inevitably establish a body of precedents on which the Negro as a citizen of the United States can take a firm stand." [27] Between these extremes is the opinion which has held that legal victories serve merely as " a barometer of public opinion " to test the " social weather " in order to determine what rights and privileges majority opinion is willing to extend to Negroes.[28]

While there is a wide gulf between court victories and the translation of such victories into practical benefits, it does appear that Negroes have received some practical benefits from their program of legal action. Discriminatory treatment remains despite court victories; but significant advantages have been de-

---

[24] 6 *University of Chicago Law Review,* 302, 303.

[25] Milton R. Konvitz, "A Nation Within a Nation, the Negro and the Supreme Court," *American Scholar,* XI (1941), 69.

[26] Gunnar Myrdal, *An American Dilemma,* I, 19; Kilpatrick, *loc. cit.,* 417 f.

[27] James W. Johnson, "Legal Aspects of the Negro Problem," *Annals of the American Academy of Political and Social Science,* CXL (1928), 97; also Scovel Richardson, "Changing Concepts of the Supreme Court as They Affect the Legal Status of the Negro," 1 *National Bar Journal,* 129.

[28] Charles H. Thompson, "Court Action the Only Reasonable Alternative to Remedy Abuses in the Negro Separate School," *Journal of Negro Education,* IV (1935), 425.

rived from favorable decisions concerning equal educational opportunities and facilities under the "equal protection" clause of the Fourteenth Amendment. Educational advancement on the graduate and professional level of the past ten years was due almost entirely to court action. It appears something more than a coincidence that school facilities for Negroes tend to be more nearly equal to those provided for white students in areas where there has been the greatest amount of litigation on the subject.[29] Such benefits have been made possible by the liberal application of the doctrine of "substantial equality" by the Supreme Court in recent years.

Hardly less significant than the benefits accruing in regard to educational opportunities was the enlarged protection for Negroes accused of crime. Court application of the "due process" clause offered protection against arbitrary treatment by state officers. Under the liberalized interpretation of due process, as applied by the Supreme Court in recent years, federal protection has been afforded throughout the entire criminal proceedings from arrest through trial. This, it seems, offers Negroes in southern states a great deal more security against arbitrary and prejudicial treatment than had heretofore obtained.

While some states have been slow in paying attention to Supreme Court mandates in matters affecting the Negro under the Fourteenth Amendment, the Court has given the Negro, in recent years, much hope for a fuller protection of his constitutional rights in the future.[30] Continued liberal interpretation of the Fourteenth Amendment by the Court, together with a decrease of racial intolerance and constant vigilance on the part of the Negro, is the combination of factors that will make the Fourteenth Amendment the protective shield of constitutional and natural rights for which it was designed when incorporated into the Federal Constitution more than seventy-five years ago.

---

29 *Ibid.*

30 It has been suggested that a new federal Civil Rights Act under the Fourteenth Amendment, similar to that declared unconstitutional by the Supreme Court in 1883, would be upheld by the present liberally constituted Court. See Washington *Afro-American*, June 12, 1943, 4.

APPENDIX

SELECTED CASES INVOLVING THE FOURTEENTH AMENDMENT AND THE NEGRO, 1920–1943

Case	*Citation*	*Date*	*State*	*Issue*	*Favorable Decision**
So. Covington & Cinn. Ry. v. Commonwealth	205 S. W. 603	1920	Ky.	Seg. interstate carrier	No
Prioleau v. U. S.	257 U. S. 633	1921	D. C.	Exclusion from jury	No
Parmalee v. Morris	218 Mich. 330	1922	Mich.	Restrictive covenant	No
Moore v. Dempsey	261 U. S. 86	1923	Ark.	Fair trial	Yes
Chandler v. Neff	298 Fed. 515	1924	Tex.	White primary	No
Corrigan v. Buckley	271 U. S. 323	1926	D. C.	Restrictive covenant	No
Wyatt v. Adair	110 So. 801	1926	Ala.	Restrictive covenant	No
Greathouse v. Bd. of School Comm.	151 N. E. 411	1926	Ind.	Educa. Seg.	No
Harmon v. Tyler	273 U. S. 668	1927	La.	Seg. ordinance	Yes
Nixon v. Herndon	273 U. S. 536	1927	Tex.	White primary	Yes
State v. Frazier	140 S. E. 324	1927	W.Va.	Exclusion from jury	Yes
Grigsby v. Harris	27 Fed. (2d) 942	1928	Tex.	White primary	No
City of Dallas v. Liberty Annex Corp.	295 S. W. 59	1929	Tex.	Seg. ordinance	Yes
West v. Bliley	33 Fed. (2d) 177	1929	Va.	White primary	Yes
City of Rich. v. Deans	37 Fed. (2d) 712	1930	Va.	Seg. ordinance	Yes
White v. Lubbock	30 S. W. 722	1930	Tex.	White primary	No
Robinson v. Holman	26 S. W. (2d) 66	1930	Ark.	White primary	No
Crawford v. U. S.	41 Fed. (2d) 979	1930	D. C.	Prej. jury	No
Aldridge v. U. S.	283 U. S. 308	1931	D. C.	Prej. jury	Yes
Downer v. Dunaway	53 Fed. 586	1931	Ga.	Fair trial	Yes
State ex rel. Cheeks v. Wirt	177 N. E. 441	1931	Ind.	Educa. seg.	No

(*Continued*)

* Indicates decision favorable to Negro litigant or Negro interest.

Case	Citation	Date	State	Issue	Favorable Decision
Nixon v. Condon	286 U. S. 73	1932	Tex.	White primary	Yes
White v. Co. Exec. Comm. of Harris County	60 Fed. (2d) 973	1932	Tex.	White primary	No
Co. Dem. Exec. Comm. of Bexar Co. v. Booker	53 S. W. (2d) 123	1932	Tex.	White primary	No
Lee v. State	161 Atl. 284	1932	Md.	Exclusion from jury	Yes
Powell v. Alabama	287 U. S. 46	1932	Ala.	Right of counsel	Yes
Hale v. Crawford	65 Fed. (2d) 739	1933	Va.	Exclusion from jury	No
Drake v. Exec. Comm. Dem. Party of Houston	2 Fed. Supp. 486	1933	Tex.	White primary	No
Trudeau v. Bonds	65 Fed. (2d) 563	1933	La.	Suffrage qualifications	No
Allen v. Okla. City	52 Pac. (2d) 1055	1935	Okla.	Seg. ordinance	Yes
Scott v. Watt	52 Pac. (2d) 1059	1935	Okla.	Seg. ordinance	Yes
Jones v. Okla. City	78 Fed. (2d) 860	1935	Okla.	Seg. ordinance	No
Ex parte Lee	52 Pac. (2d) 1059	1935	Okla.	Seg. ordinance	Yes
Patterson v. Alabama	294 U. S. 587	1935	Ala.	Exclusion from jury	Yes
Norris v. Alabama	294 U. S. 600	1935	Ala.	Exclusion from jury	Yes
Hollins v. Oklahoma	295 U. S. 394	1935	Okla.	Fair trial	Yes
Grovey v. Townsend	295 U. S. 45	1935	Tex.	White primary	No
Univ. of Md. v. Murray	169 Md. 478	1936	Md.	Admiss. Negro to state univ.	Yes
Brown v. Mississippi	297 U. S. 278	1936	Miss.	Coerced confess.	Yes
Rounds v. State	106 S. W. (2d) 212	1937	Tenn.	Coerced confess.	Yes
State v. Logan	111 S. W. (2d) 110	1937	Mo.	Exclusion from jury	Yes
Herndon v. Lowry	301 U. S. 242	1937	Ga.	Free speech	Yes
Williams v. Zimmerman	192 Atl. 353	1937	Md.	Educa. seg.	No
Hale v. Kentucky	303 U. S. 613	1938	Ky.	Exclusion from jury	Yes
Mo. ex rel. Gaines v. Canada	305 U. S. 337	1938	Mo.	Admiss. Negro to state univ.	Yes
Mills v. Bd. of Ed. of Anne Arundel Co.	30 Fed. Supp. 245	1939	Md.	Salary discrim.	Yes

(*Continued*)

Case	*Citation*	*Date*	*State*	*Issue*	*Favorable Decision*
Pierre v. Louisiana	306 U. S. 354	1939	La.	Exclusion from jury	Yes
Carruthers v. Reed	102 Fed. (2d) 933	1939	Ark.	Fair trial	No
Canty v. Alabama	309 U. S. 629	1940	Ala.	Coerced confess.	Yes
Clinard v. City Winston Salem	6 S. E. (2d) 867	1940	N. C.	Seg. ordinance	Yes
Chambers v. Florida	309 U. S. 227	1940	Fla.	Coerced confess.	Yes
U. S. v. Sutherland	37 Fed. Supp. 344	1940	Ga.	Coerced confess.	Yes
White v. Texas	309 U. S. 631	1940	Tex.	Coerced confess.	Yes
Smith v. Texas	311 U. S. 128	1940	Tex.	Exclusion from jury	Yes
Alston v. School Bd. City of Norfolk	112 Fed. (2d) 992	1940	Va.	Salary discrim.	Yes
Bluford v. Canada	32 Fed. Supp. 707	1940	Mo.	Admiss. Negro to state univ.	No
Hansberry v. Lee	311 U. S. 32	1940	Ill.	Restrictive covenant	Yes
Favors v. Randall	40 Fed. Supp. 743	1941	Pa.	Seg. public housing	No
McDaniel v. Bd. of Pub. Instr. Escombia Co.	39 Fed. Supp. 638	1941	Fla.	Salary discrim.	Yes
Wilcoxon v. Aldridge	15 S. E. (2d) 873	1941	Ga.	Right of counsel	Yes
Lomax v. Texas	313 U. S. 544	1941	Tex.	Coerced confess.	Yes
Vernon v. Alabama	313 U. S. 547	1941	Ala.	Coerced confess.	Yes
Mitchell v. U. S.	313 U. S. 80	1941	Ark.	Seg. interstate carrier	Yes
Thomas v. Hibbetts	46 Fed. Supp. 368	1942	Tenn.	Salary discrim.	Yes
Coates v. State	25 Atl. (2d) 676	1942	Md.	Right of counsel	Yes
Ward v. Texas	316 U. S. 547	1942	Tex.	Coerced confess.	Yes
Hill v. Texas	316 U. S. 400	1942	Tex.	Exclusion from jury	Yes
State v. Grant	19 S. E. (2d) 638	1942	S. C.	Exclusion from jury	No
U. S. ex rel. Jackson v. Brady	132 Fed. (2d) 476	1943	Md.	Exclusion from jury	No

BIBLIOGRAPHY

OFFICIAL SOURCES

Atlantic Reporter: 161, 192; second series, 25.

Federal Reporter: 10, 298; second series, 27, 31, 33, 37, 53, 60, 65, 78, 102, 112, 132.

Federal Supplement: 2, 30, 32, 37, 39, 40, 46.

Maryland Code Annotated, Baltimore, 1939.

Maryland, Commission on Scholarships for Negroes, *Special Report to the Governor and Legislature,* Baltimore, 1939.

Maryland Reports: 169.

Missouri, *Revised Statutes,* Jefferson City, 1939.

Missouri Statutes Annotated, St. Paul, 1932.

National Association for the Advancement of Colored People, *Annual Reports,* 1920–1943, New York, 1921–1944.

North Carolina, Commission to Study Public Schools and Colleges for Colored People, *Report and Recommendations,* Raleigh, 1938.

Northeastern Reporter: 151, 177.

Northwestern Reporter: 188.

Pacific Reporter: 226; second series, 52.

Southern Reporter: 110.

Southeastern Reporter: 140; second series, 15, 19, 65.

Southwestern Reporter: 205, 295; second series, 26, 30, 53, 106, 111.

U. S. Bureau of the Census, *Abstract of the Fourteenth Census of the United States,* 1920, Washington, 1923.

U. S. Bureau of the Census, *Fifteenth Census of the United States,* 1930, *Population,* Washington, 1933.

U. S. Bureau of the Census, *Negro Population, 1790–1915,* Washington, 1918.

U. S. *Congressional Record,* 1920, 1928, Washington, 1921, 1929.

United States Reports: 100, 109, 118, 163, 177, 200, 245, 257, 261, 271, 273, 275, 283, 286, 287, 294, 295, 297, 301, 303, 305, 306, 309,310, 311, 313, 316.

U. S. Senate, Subcommittee on the Judiciary, *Hearing on S. 291: A Bill Creating a Commission on the Racial Question.*

SECONDARY MATERIAL

Books

Adriaans, John H., *Has the Negro a Right to Vote?,* Washington, 1908.

Allen, James S., *The Negro Question in the United States,* New York, 1935.

American Civil Liberties Union, *Black Justice,* New York, 1931.

Baker, Paul E., *Negro-White Adjustment,* Pittsfield, Mass., 1934.

Bates, E. S., *The Story of the Supreme Court,* Indianapolis, 1936.

Blaine, James G., *Twenty Years of Congress,* Norwich, Conn., 1886, 2 v.

Bond, Horace M., *The Education of the Negro in the American Social Order,* New York, 1934.

Burgess, John W., *Reconstruction and the Constitution, 1866–1876,* New York, 1902.

Chambliss, Rollins, *What Some Negro Newspapers of Georgia Say About Some Social Problems, 1933,* Athens, Georgia, 1934.

Collins, Charles W., *The Fourteenth Amendment and the States,* Boston, 1912.

Dabney, Virginius, *Liberalism in the South,* Chapel Hill, 1933.

Dillard, Irving, *Mr. Justice Brandeis, Great American,* St. Louis, 1941.

Duncan Hannibal, *The Changing Race Relations in the Border and Northern States,* Philadelphia, 1922.

Embree, Edwin R., *Julius Rosenwald Fund, 1942–1944,* Chicago, 1944.

Ewing, C. A. M., *The Judges of the Supreme Court, 1789–1937,* Minneapolis, 1938.

Flack, Horace E., *The Adoption of the Fourteenth Amendment,* Baltimore, 1908.

Frankfurter, Felix, *Mr. Justice Holmes and the Constitution,* Cambridge, Mass., 1927.

———, *Mr. Justice Holmes and the Supreme Court,* Cambridge, Mass., 1938.

Green, John R., *Liberty Under the Fourteenth Amendment,* St. Louis, 1942.

Guthrie, William D., *The Fourteenth Article of Amendment to the Constitution of the United States,* Boston, 1898.

Hallowell, R. P., *Why the Negro Was Enfranchised: Negro Suffrage Justified,* Boston, 1903.

Haynes, George E., *Negro Migration and Its Implications North and South,* New York, 1923.

Jack, Robert E., *History of the National Association for the Advancement of Colored People,* Boston, 1943.

Henderson, Donald H., *The Urbanization of the American Negro,* New Haven, 1937.

Johnson, Charles S., *Patterns of Negro Segregation,* New York, 1943.

———, *The Negro in American Civilization,* New York, 1930.

Jones, John J., *The Negroes Are an Economic Problem, Not a Race Problem,* New York, 1933.

Jones, Lance G., *Negro Schools in the Southern States,* Oxford, 1928.

Kennedy, Louise V., *The Negro Peasant Turns Cityward,* New York, 1930.

Klineberg, Otto, *Negro Intelligence and Selective Migration,* New York, 1935.

Klinkhamer, O.P., Sr. Marie Carolyn, *Edward Douglas White,* Washington, 1943.

Knight, Charles L., *Negro Housing in Certain Virginia Cities,* Richmond, 1927.

Lewinson, Paul, *Race, Class and Party,* New York, 1942.

Logan, Rayford, *The Attitude of the Southern Press Toward Negro Suffrage, 1932–1940,* Washington, 1940.

Long, H. L., *Public Secondary Education for Negroes in North Carolina,* New York, 1932.

Mabry, William A., *Studies in the Disfranchisement of the Negro in the South,* Durham, 1938.

Mangum, Charles S., *The Legal Status of the Negro,* Chapel Hill, 1940.

Martin, Robert E., *Negro Disfranchisement in Virginia,* Washington, 1938.

Mason, Alpheus, *Brandeis: Lawyer and Judge in the Modern State,* Princeton, 1933.

McGuinn, Henry J., *The Courts and the Changing Status of Negroes in Maryland,* Richmond, 1940.

Meece, Leonard, *Negro Education in Kentucky,* Lexington, Ky., 1938.

Morton, Richard L., *The Negro in Virginia Politics, 1865–1902,* Charlottesville, Va., 1919.

Myrdal, Gunnar, *An American Dilemma,* New York, 1944, 2 v.

National Association for the Advancement of Colored People, *Teachers' Salaries in Black and White,* New York, 1942.

President's Conference on Home Building and Home Ownership, Committee on Negro Housing, *Negro Housing,* Washington, 1932.

President's Research Committee on Social Trends, *Recent Social Trends in the United States,* New York, 1933.

Porter, Kirk, *A History of Suffrage in the United States,* Chicago, 1918.

Risen, Maurice L., *Legal Aspects of Segregation of the Races in Public Schools,* Philadelphia, 1935.

Stephenson, G. T., *Race Distinctions in American Law,* New York, 1910.

Styles, F. L., *Negroes and the Law,* Boston, 1937.

U. S. National Commission on Law Observance and Law Enforcement, *Lawlessness and Law Enforcement,* Washington, 1931.

U. S. Office of Education, *National Survey of Higher Education for Negroes,* Washington, 1942, 3 v.

Van Deusen, John G., *The Black Man in White America,* Washington, 1944.

Warren, Charles, *The Supreme Court in United States History,* Boston, 1935, 2 v.

Wilkerson, Doxey, *Special Problems of Negro Education,* Washington, 1939.

Woofter, Thomas J., *Negro Housing in Philadelphia,* Philadelphia, 1927.

———, *Negro Problems in Cities,* New York, 1928.

Young, Donald, *American Minority Peoples,* New York, 1932.

———, *Minority Peoples in the Depression,* New York, 1937.

Periodicals

Adams, Charles Francis, "Reflex Light from Africa," *Century Magazine,* LXXII (May, 1906), 101–111.

Ajootian, George, "The Right of Negroes to Vote in State Primaries," 12 *Boston University Law Review,* 689–694.

Alexander, W. W., "Progress in Interracial Cooperation," *Missionary Review of the World,* XLV (January, 1922), 469–472; "Racial Good Will Movements," *Missionary Review of the World,* XLVII (July, 1924), 505–512.

Alilunas, Leo, "Legal Restrictions on the Negro in Politics," *Journal of Negro History,* XXV (April, 1940), 153–202; "Statutory Means of Impeding Emigration of the Negro," *Journal of Negro History,* XXII (April, 1937), 148–162.

Armistead, H. M., "Racial Exclusion in Jury Trials," Arkansas Bar Association, *Proceedings,* 1933, 99–115.

"Attack on the Fourteenth Amendment," 18 *Lawyer and Banker,* 19–27.

Baker, G. W., "The Trend of United States Supreme Court Decisions as Affecting Negro Rights," 1 *National Bar Journal,* 30–37.

Barbour, J. F., "Exclusion of Negroes from Jury Service," 8 *Mississippi Law Journal,* 196–205.

Barksdale, N. P., "The Gaines Case and Its Effect on Negro Education in Missouri," *School and Society,* LI (March, 1940), 309–313.

Bates, Thelma, "The Legal Status of the Negro in Florida," *Florida Historical Society Quarterly,* VI (January, 1928), 159–181.

Bond, Horace M., "The Extent and Character of Separate Schools in the United States," *Journal of Negro Education,* IV (July, 1935), 321–327.

Booth, Betty, "Sufficiency of Evidence to Establish Discrimination," 30 *Journal of Criminal Law,* 264–266.

Boudin, Louis B., "Truth and Fiction About the Fourteenth Amendment," 16 *New York University Law Quarterly Review,* 19–82.

Brown, W. O., "Interracial Cooperation: Some of Its Problems," *Opportunity,* XI (September, 1933), 272–273, 285.

Bruce, A. A., "Racial Zoning by Private Contract in the Light of the Constitution and the Rule Against Restraints on Alienation," 21 *Illinois Law Review,* 704–717.

Bunche, Ralph J., "Tactics and Programs of Minority Groups," *Journal of Negro Education,* IV (July, 1935), 308–320.

Burcham, Joseph R., "Discrimination Against Negroes in Primary Elections," 12 *St. Louis Law Review,* 199–204.

Burgess, Ernest W., "Residential Segregation in American Cities," *Annals of the American Society of Political and Social Science,* CXL (November, 1928), 105–115.

Burgess, John W., "Present Problems of Constitutional Law," *Political Science Quarterly,* XIX (December, 1904), 545–578.

Calverton, V. E., "The Negro's New Belligerent Attitude," *Current History,* XXX (September, 1929), 1081–1088.

Chafee, Z., "Liberal Trends in the Supreme Court," *Current History,* XXXV (December, 1931), 338–344.

Chamberlin, John B., "The Validity of Texas Legislation Limiting Voting at Primaries," 27 *Illinois Law Review,* 686–688.

Chirgwin, A. M., "Negro Race Movements in America," *Contemporary Review,* CXXVII (February, 1925), 200–206.

Cidella, A. J. and Kaplan, I. J., "Discrimination Against Negroes in Jury Service," 29 *Illinois Law Review,* 498–506.

Collins, Charles W., "The Failure of the Fourteenth Amendment as a Constitutional Idea," *South Atlantic Quarterly,* XI (April, 1912), 105–115; "The Fourteenth Amendment and the Negro Race Question," 45 *American Law Review,* 830–856.

Davis, P. O., "Negro Exodus and Southern Agriculture," *Review of Reviews,* LXVIII (October, 1923), 401–407.

Donelson, Lewis, "Enforceability of Restrictive Covenants on Land in the District of Columbia," 29 *Georgetown Law Journal,* 500–509.

Drake, F. B., "The Negro Before the Supreme Court," 66 *Albany Law Journal,* 238–248.

DuBois, W. E. B., "The Defeat of Judge Parker," *Crisis,* XXXVII (July, 1930), 225–227.

"Due Process of Law in Arkansas," *New Republic,* XXXIV (March, 1923), 55–57.

Evans, L. H., "Primary Elections and the Constitution," 32 *Michigan Law Review,* 451–477.

"Exclusion of Negroes From Juries," 1 *Louisiana Law Review,* 841–846.

"Exploitation that is Getting Dangerous," *World Outlook,* V (October, 1919), 14–15.

Felman, A. J., "Racial Discrimination in the Party Primary," 8 *New York University Law Quarterly Review,* 309–313.

Fergenbaum, Joseph, "Political Discrimination by Party Control over Primary Elections," 17 *St. Louis Law Review,* 155–163.

Gardner, M., "Race Segregation in Cities," 29 *Kentucky Law Journal,* 213–219.

Garner, James W., "The Fourteenth Amendment and Southern Representation," *South Atlantic Quarterly,* IV (July, 1905), 209–216.

Graham, Howard J., "The Conspiracy Theory of the Fourteenth Amendment," 47 *Yale Law Journal,* 371–403, 48 *Yale Law Journal,* 171–194.

Gressman, E., "Jurisdiction of Federal Courts over Violation of Civil Liberties by State Governments and by Private Individuals," 39 *Michigan Law Review,* 284–297.

Hainsworth, R. W., "The Negro and the Texas Primaries," *Journal of Negro History,* XVIII (October, 1933), 426–450.

Hamilton, W. H., "The Legal Philosophy of Justices Holmes and Brandeis," *Current History,* XXXIII (February, 1931), 654–660.

Henderson, Donald, "The Negro Migration of 1916–1918," *Journal of Negro History,* VI (October, 1921), 383–498.

Holt, G. D., "The Constitutionality of Municipal Zoning and Segregation Ordinances," 33 *West Virginia Law Quarterly,* 332–349.

Hooper, Alexander, "The Negro and the Fourteenth Amendment," *Harper's Weekly,* XLVIII (March, 1904), 438.

Jefferson, Bernard S., "Race Discrimination in Jury Service," 19 *Boston University Law Review,* 413–447.

Johnson, Guy B., "Negro Racial Movements and Leadership in the United States," *American Journal of Sociology,* XLIII (July, 1937), 57–71; "Some Factors in the Development of Negro Social Institutions in the United States," *American Journal of Sociology,* XL (November, 1934), 329–337.

Johnson, James W., "Legal Aspects of the Negro Problem," *Annals of the American Academy of Political and Social Science,* CXL (November, 1928), 90–97; "The Negro Looks at Politics," *American Mercury,* XVIII (September, 1929), 88–94.

Jones, Harry H., "The Negro Before the Courts During 1932," *Crisis,* XL (September, 1933), 206, 214.

Kievets, E., "Equal Protection: Negro Educational Facilities," 13 *Southern California Law Review,* 68–75.

Kilpatrick, W. H., "Resort to Courts by Negroes to Improve Their School a Conditional Alternative," *Journal of Negro Education,* IV (July, 1935), 412–418.

Konvitz, Milton R., "A Nation Within a Nation—the Negro and the Supreme Court," *American Scholar,* XI (January, 1941), 69–78.

Lee, E. T., "Should Not the Fourteenth Amendment to the Constitution of the United States Be Amended?", 42 *Commercial Law Journal,* 67–71.

"The Legality of Race Segregation in Educational Institutions," 82 *University of Pennsylvania Law Review,* 157–164.

Martin, A. T., "The Segregation of Residences of Negroes," 32 *Michigan Law Review,* 721–742.

Maxey, Edwin, "The Enforcement of the Fourteenth Amendment," 66 *Albany Law Journal,* 274–276.

McGuinn, Henry J., "Equal Protection of the Law and Fair Trials in Maryland," *Journal of Negro History,* XXIV (April, 1939), 143–166.

McKee, O., "The Liberal Supreme Court," *Outlook,* CLIX (October, 1931), 171–173.

McLaughlin, Andrew C., "The Court, the Corporation and Conkling," *American Historical Review,* XLVI (October, 1940), 45–63.

McQuillan, E., "The Constitutional Validity of Zoning Under the Police Power," 11 *St. Louis Law Review,* 76–107.

Mencken, H. L., "Notes on Negro Strategy," *Crisis,* XLI (October, 1934), 289, 304.

Miller, Kelly, "Government and the Negro," *Annals of the American Academy of Political and Social Science,* CXL (November, 1928), 98–104; "Is the Color Line Crumbling?", *Opportunity,* VII (September, 1929), 282–285; "Separate Communities for Negroes," *Current History,* XXV (March, 1927), 827–833.

Milman, M., "The Right of Negroes to Vote in State Primaries," 15 *Cornell Law Quarterly*, 262–269.

Murphy, Edgar G., "Should the Fourteenth Amendment Be Enforced?" *North American Review*, CLXXX (January, 1905), 109–133.

"The Negro Citizen in the Supreme Court," 52 *Harvard Law Review*, 823–832.

Nutting, C. B., "The Supreme Court, the Fourteenth Amendment, and State Criminal Cases," 3 *University of Chicago Law Review*, 244–260.

Owsley, F. L., "Scottsboro, the Third Crusade: Sequel to Abolition and Reconstruction," *American Review*, I (June, 1933), 257–285.

Peckstein, L. A., "The Problem of Negro Education in Northern and Border Cities," *Elementary School Journal*, XXX (November, 1929), 172–199.

Peterson, Gladys T., "The Present Status of the Negro Separate School as Defined by Court Decisions," *Journal of Negro Education*, IV (July, 1935), 351–374.

Pollard, John P., "Hughes the Humanitarian," *North American Review*, CCXXIX (April, 1930), 444–448; "Justice Brandeis and the Constitution," *Scribner's Magazine*, LXXXVII (January, 1930), 11–19; "Justice Holmes Dissents," *Scribner's Magazine*, LXXXV (January, 1929), 22–29; "Our Supreme Court Goes Liberal," *Forum*, LXXXVI (October, 1931), 193–199.

Purcell, Richard J., "Mr. Justice Pierce Butler," *Catholic Educational Review*, XLII (April, June, September, 1944), 193–215, 327–341, 420–432.

Quindry, F. E., "Airline Passenger Discrimination," 3 *Journal of Air Law*, 479–514.

"Race Equality by Statute," 84 *University of Pennsylvania Law Review*, 75–84.

Ribble, F. D., "Legal Restraints on the Choice of a Dwelling," 78 *University of Pennsylvania Law Review*, 842–853.

Richardson, Scovel, "Changing Concepts of the Supreme Court as They Affect the Legal Status of Negroes," 1 *National Bar Journal*, 113–129.

"The Right of Political Parties to Exclude Negroes from Party Primaries," 16 *Virginia Law Review*, 193–197.

"The Rising Tide of Negro Protest," *Christian Century*, XLVII (September, 1930), 1140–1141.

Ryan, J. A., "Due Process and Mr. Justice Black," *Catholic World*, CLI (April, 1940), 36–39.

Sandmeyer, Elmer C., "California Anti-Chinese Legislation and the Federal Courts," *Pacific Historical Review*, V (January, 1936), 189–211.

Schaal, E. A., "Will the Negro Rely on Force?", *Crisis*, XL (January, 1933), 8–9.

"Scottsboro, What Now?", *New Republic*, LXXXII (April, 1935), 270–271.

Seligmann, Herbert J., "The Negro's Influence as a Voter," *Current History,* XXVIII (May, 1928), 230–231; "The Negro and the Supreme Court," *Forum,* LXXXVI (December, 1931), Supp. 24.

Simms., Newell L., "Techniques of Race Adjustment," *Journal of Negro History,* XVI (January, 1931), 79–87.

Snyder, H., "Negro Migration and the Cotton Crop," *North American Review,* CCXIX (January, 1924), 2–29.

Standing, T. G., "Nationalism in Negro Leadership," *American Journal of Sociology,* XL (September, 1934), 180–192.

Stolinski, A. S., "Legal Effects of a Contract or Covenant in Relation to Real Property Which Discriminates Against Persons Because of Race or Color," 8 *Bi-Monthly Law Review,* 45–64.

Strout, R. L., "The New Deal and the Supreme Court," *North American Review,* CCXXXVI (December, 1933), 484–491.

Sugarman, Joseph, "The Right to Counsel," 13 *Boston University Law Review,* 92–98.

Van Deusen, John, "The Negro in Politics," *Journal of Negro History,* XXI (July, 1936), 256–274.

Villard, Oswald G., "The Crumbling Color Line," *Harper's Magazine,* CLIX (July, 1929), 156–167.

Walrond, E. D., "The Negro Exodus from the South," *Current History Magazine,* XVIII (September, 1923), 292–294.

Warsoff, L. A., "The Weight of the Presumption of Constitutionality under the Fourteenth Amendment," 18 *Boston University Law Review,* 319–341.

Weeks, C. D., "The White Primary," 8 *Mississippi Law Journal,* 135–153.

Wesley, Charles H., "The Historical Basis of Negro Citizenship," *Opportunity,* II (December, 1924), 356–359.

White, Walter, "The Negro and the Supreme Court," *Harper's Magazine,* CLXII (January, 1931), 238–246; "Negro Segregation Comes North," *Nation,* CXXI (October, 1925), 458–460.

Windolph, F. L., "Two Fourteenth Amendments," *Annals of the American Society of Political and Social Science,* CXCV (January, 1938), 268–283.

Woodson, C. G., "Fifty Years of Negro Citizenship as Qualified by the United States Supreme Court," *Journal of Negro History,* VI (January, 1921), 1–53.

Unpublished Essays

Ackiss, Thelma D., "The Negro and the Supreme Court to 1900," master's thesis, Howard University, 1936.

Holloway, Charles S., "The Fourteenth Amendment and Negro Education," master's thesis, Catholic University of America, 1942.

Martin, Lou E., "The Effect of Court Decisions on Negro Education in the South," master's thesis, Howard University, 1935.

Minnis, Fred, "The Attitude of Federal Courts on the Exclusion of Negroes from Jury Service," master's thesis, Howard University, 1934.

Peterson, Gladys T., "The Courts and the Negro Public School," master's thesis, Howard University, 1934.

Newspapers

Atlanta *Daily World,* April 1, 1933; April 6, 1933.

Baltimore *Sun,* November 29, 1939.

Birmingham *News,* November 7, 1932; April 5, 1935; April 20, 1935; April 30, 1935.

Chicago *Defender,* September 26, 1942; October 16, 1943; October 30, 1943; January 29, 1944; February 5, 1944; February 12, 1944; February 26, 1944; March 4, 1944; May 12, 1944.

Dallas *Morning News,* May 4, 1932; June 2, 1942.

Galveston *Daily News,* April 6, 1924; March 8, 1927; May 4, 1932.

Houston *Post-Dispatch,* March 8, 1927; May 4, 1932.

Jackson (Miss.) *Daily Clarion-Ledger,* February 18, 1936.

Little Rock (Ark.) *Arkansas Democrat,* June 26, 1934.

Little Rock (Ark.) *Arkansas Gazette,* February 20, 1923; February 21, 1923.

New Orleans *States,* March 14, 1927.

New Orleans *Times-Picayune,* March 15, 1927.

New York *Herald-Tribune,* November 8, 1932; April 29, 1941.

New York *Sun,* March 8, 1932; April 29, 1941.

New York *Times,* December 6, 1920; September 12, 1922; January 6, 1925; November 1, 1925; December 29, 1925; March 17, 1926; May 25, 1926; June 1, 1926; March 8, 1927; March 15, 1927; January 8, 1928; December 8, 1929; February 14, 1931; July 12, 1932; November 6, 1932; November 13, 1932; April 2, 1933; April 26, 1933; April 5, 1935; April 7, 1935; April 9, 1935; November 12, 1939; April 27, 1941.

Norfolk *Journal and Guide,* February 25, 1933; August 12, 1933; October 12, 1933; December 23, 1933; April 6, 1935; April 13, 1935; April 27, 1935; May 4, 1935; May 11, 1935; May 25, 1935; June 22, 1935; July 6, 1935; July 27, 1935; August 17, 1935; August 31, 1935; March 6, 1937; April 24, 1937; May 1, 1937; May 15, 1937; October 16, 1937; October 23, 1937; January 8, 1938; October 8, 1938; November 5, 1938; December 17, 1938; December 24, 1938; January 7, 1939; February 11, 1939; June 14, 1939; June 29, 1940; January 24, 1942; April 18, 1942; August 1, 1942; October 10, 1942; July 24, 1943; October 23, 1943; December 18, 1943.

Oklahoma City *Daily Oklahoman,* May 14, 1935; November 27, 1935.

Pittsburgh *Courier,* January 25, 1930; April 25, 1931; May 1, 1943; June 26, 1943; January 29, 1944.

Richmond *Times-Dispatch,* June 6, 1929; June 12, 1933; June 17, 1933; April 3, 1935; December 15, 1938; June 21, 1940.

San Antonio *Express,* April 6, 1924; May 4, 1932; June 1, 1932.

Tulsa *Daily News,* May 14, 1935.

Washington *Afro-American,* April 22, 1933; April 29, 1933; May 6, 1933; November 1, 1933; May 11, 1935; June 22, 1935; November 9, 1935; February 22, 1936; February 13, 1937; March 6, 1937; March 27, 1937; May 1, 1937; July 31, 1937; September 11, 1937; September 25, 1937; October 2, 1937; June 11, 1938; January 21, 1939; February 11, 1939; April 1, 1939; July 8, 1939; August 12, 1939; September 23, 1939; January 6, 1940; March 10, 1940; March 30, 1940; March 1, 1941; May 3, 1941; May 10, 1941; August 9, 1941; October 11, 1941; February 28, 1942; January 13, 1943; June 12, 1943; October 30, 1943; April 5, 1944; May 1, 1944.

Washington *Post,* May 25, 1926.

INDEX